The Best Places
To Kiss™
In Northern California

The Best Places
To Kiss™
In Northern California

by Paula Begoun & Tomi Jo Taylor
Beginning Press

Art Direction & Production: Constance Bollen
Cover Design: Rob Pawlak
Typography: Common Line Communications
Editor: Phyllis Hatfield
Printing: Bookcrafters
Contributors: Avis Begoun

Copyright 1990 by Paula Begoun
Beginning Press, 5418 South Brandon, Seattle, Washington 98118
First Edition: June 1990
    3 4 5 6 7 8 9 10

Best Places To Kiss™ is a registered trademark of Beginning Press ISBN 0-9615514-7-X

This book may be ordered directly from the publisher:
Beginning Press, 5418 South Brandon, Seattle, Washington 98118

Please include $9.95 ($12.95 Canandian) plus $1.50 postage and handling.

Professional Thank Yous

Thanks to Barbara Murel and Michael Hofferbert for their typesetting skills and patience, Constance Bollen for her book designing expertise, and to Phyllis Hatfield whose quick (*very quick*) and succint editing skills were greatly appreciated.

Special Acknowledgments

To Avis Begoun, for the very creative original idea for this book, Dorothy Roer for her lifesaving last-minute assistance and supportive friendship, and to all the starry-eyed Northern Californians who offered their valuable suggestions that helped us find the kissing places included in this collection.

Publisher's Note

    This book is **not** an advertising vehicle. As was true in all the Best Places To Kiss books, none of the businesses included here was told it either was being considered or had been chosen for inclusion; establishments were neither charged fees nor did they pay us. No services were exchanged. This book is a sincere effort to highlight those special parts of the area that are filled with romance and splendor. Sometimes those places are created by people, as in restaurants, inns, lounges, lodges, hotels and bed & breakfasts. Sometimes those places are untouched by people and simply created by G-d for us to enjoy.

    The recommendations in this collection were the final decision of the publisher. Please write to Beginning Press if you have any additional comments, suggestions or recommendations.

"As usual with most lovers in the city —
they were troubled by the lack of that
essential need of love — a meeting place."

Thomas Wolfe

Dedication

To my sister Avis, who helps me see inside myself so that it is easier to love without judgments and fear.

> "THE SOUND OF A KISS IS NOT SO LOUD AS
> THAT OF A CANNON — BUT ITS ECHO LASTS
> A GREAT DEAL LONGER."
>
> *Oliver Wendell Holmes, Sr.*

TABLE OF CONTENTS

"TO WRITE A GOOD LOVE LETTER, YOU OUGHT
TO BEGIN WITHOUT KNOWING WHAT YOU MEAN TO
SAY AND TO FINISH WITHOUT KNOWING
WHAT YOU HAVE WRITTEN."

Jean Jacques Rousseau

KISSING 101

Why Is It Best To Kiss In Northern California?

I've wondered about why it's best to kiss in a particular city from the moment I started writing this series of romantic travel guides. I began with the original Pacific Northwest kissing book three years ago (it has since been updated), and I have completed three others — one for the Southern California area, one for New York City and now this one for Northern California. In each area I ask this same question and hope that before I'm done I will have found an answer. For Northern California the answer came easy.

There probably is not a more diverse yet compact place in the world in which to pucker up. San Francisco, the Bay Area, and the majestic destinations a short drive north, south and east — all will ignite your imaginations and passions. If you've ever longed for that special place where you can share closeness, you can find it here. Wine tastings, bed & breakfasts, hot air balloon rides, vibrant nightlife, alluring restaurants, country hikes, lofty woods, city streets filled with extravagant shopping, expansive parks, not to mention the ocean and bridges and valleys and entertainment and...in short, Northern California is an adult carnival. From shore to valley, the vitality and romance here are contagious, and when you're accompanied by the right someone, the only challenge will be to find the lovable niche that serves your hearts best.

You Call This Research?

This book was undertaken primarily as a journalistic effort. It is the product of earnest interviews, travel, careful investigation and observation. Although it would have been nice, actually even preferable, kissing was not used as the major research method for selecting the locations listed in this book. If smooching had been the determining factor, several inescapable problems would have developed. First, I assure you, we would still be researching, and this book would be just a good idea, some breathless moments, random notes and nothing more. And depending on the mood of the moment, many kisses would have occurred in a lot of places that do not meet the requirements of this travel guide. Therefore, for both practical and physical reasons, a more objective criterion had to be established.

By now you may be wondering, if we did not kiss at every location during our research, how could we be certain if a particular place was good for such an activity? The answer is that we employed our reporters' instincts to evaluate the heartfelt, magnetic pull of each place visited. If, upon examining a place, we felt a longing inside for our special someone to share what we had discovered, we considered this to be as reliable as a kissing analysis. In the final evaluation, I can guarantee that once you choose where to go from among any of the places listed, you will be assured of some amount of privacy, a beautiful setting, heart-stirring ambience and first-rate accommodations. When you get there, what you do romantically is up to you and your partner.

What Isn't Romantic?

You may be skeptical about the idea that one location is more romantic than another. You may think, *"Well, it isn't the setting, it's who you're with that makes a place special."* And you'd be right. But aside from the chemistry that exists between the two of you without any help from us, there are some locations that can facilitate and enhance that chemistry, just as there are those that discourage and frustrate the magic in the moment.

For example, holding hands over a hamburger and fries at McDonald's, might be, for some, a blissful interlude. But the french-fry fight in full swing near your heads and the preoccupied employee who took a year and a day to get your order will put a damper on heart-throb stuff for most of us, even the most adoring. No, location isn't everything; but when a certain type of place combines with all the right atmospheric details, including the right person, the odds are better for achieving unhindered and uninterrupted romance.

With that in mind, here is a list of things that were considered to be not even remotely romantic: olive green or orange carpeting (especially if it was mildewy or dirty); anything overly plastic or overly veneered; an abundance of neon (even if it was very art deco or very neo-modern); most tourist traps; restaurants with no-smoking sections who ignored their own policy; overpriced hotels with impressive names and mediocre accommodations; discos; the latest need-to-be-seen-in nightspot; restaurants with officious, sneering waiters; and last but not least, a roomful of people discussing the stock market or the hottest and latest business acquisition in town.

Above and beyond these unromantic location details, there is a small variety of unromantic behaviors that can negate the affection potential of even the most majestic surroundings. These are mood-killers every time: any amount of moaning over the weather; creating a scene over the quality of food or service, no matter how justified; worrying about work; getting angry about traffic; incessant back-seat driving, no matter how warranted; groaning about heartburn and other related symptoms, no matter how painful or justified.

Rating Romance

The three major factors that determined whether a place would be included here were:

1. **Surrounding splendor**
2. **Privacy**
3. **Tug-at-your-heartstrings ambience**

Of the three determining factors, *"surrounding splendor"* and *"privacy"* are fairly self explanatory. *"Heart-tugging ambience"* can probably use some clarification. Ambience, by our definition, is not limited to four-poster beds covered with down quilts and lace pillows, or tables decorated with white tablecloths and nicely folded linen napkins. Instead there must be more plush or other engaging features that encourage intimacy and allow for uninterrupted affectionate discussions. For the most part, ambience was rated according to degree of comfort and number of gracious appointments, as opposed to image and frills.

If a place had all three of the qualities listed above, its inclusion was automatic. If one or two of the criteria were weak or nonexistent, the other feature(s) had to be really incredible before the place would be included. For example, if a breathtakingly beautiful viewpoint was situated in an area inundated with tourists and families on vacations, the place was not included. On the other hand, if a fabulous bed & breakfast was set in a less-than-desirable location, it was included if and only if its interior was so wonderfully inviting and cozy that the outside world no longer mattered.

Kiss Ratings

If you've flipped through this book and noticed the miniature lips that follow each entry, you're probably curious about what they mean. The rating system notwithstanding, ALL the places listed in this book are wonderfully special places to be, and all of them have heart-pleasing details and are worthwhile, enticing places to visit. The tiny lips indicate only our personal preferences and nothing more. They are a way of indicating just how delightfully romantic a place is and how pleased we were with our experience during our visit. The number of lips awarded each location indicates the following:

Romantic Possibilities

💋 *Very Romantic*

💋💋 *Magical*

💋💋💋 *Irresistible*

💋💋💋💋 *Sublime*

Rating Cost

There are also additional ratings to help you determine whether your lips can afford to kiss in a particular restaurant, hotel or bed & breakfast (almost all of the outdoor places are free; some charge a small fee). The price for overnight accommodations is always based on double occupancy; otherwise there wouldn't be anyone to kiss. Eating-establishment prices are based on a full dinner for two, excluding liquor, unless otherwise indicated. Because prices and business hours change, it is always advisable to call each place you consider visiting, so that your lips do not end up disappointed.

Restaurant Rating

Very Inexpensive — Under $25
Inexpensive — $25 to $45
Moderate — $50 to $75
Expensive — $80 to $125
Very Expensive — $130 to $150
Unbelievably Expensive — $150 and up

Lodging Rating

Very Inexpensive — Under $75
Inexpensive — $80 to $90
Moderate — $90 to $125
Expensive — $130 to $175
Very Expensive — $185 to $240
Unbelievably Expensive — $250 and up

What If You Don't Want To Kiss?

Some people I interviewed resisted the idea of best-kissing locales. Their resistance stemmed from expectation worries. They were apprehensive that once they arrived at the place of their dreams, they'd never get the feeling they thought they were supposed to have.

They imagined spending time setting up itineraries, taking the extra time to get ready, making the journey to the promised land and once they were there, not being swept away in a flourish of romance. Their understandable fear was: What happens if nothing happens?

Having experienced those situations more than once in my life, I empathize, but I'm prepared with solutions. To prevent this anti-climactic scenario from becoming a reality, and to help you survive a romantic outing, consider these suggestions: When you make decisions about where and when to go, pay close attention to details; talk over your preferences and discuss your feelings about them. For some people there is no passion associated with fast pre-theatre dinners which are all but inhaled, or with walking further than expected in overly high, high heels, or with finding a place closed because their hours have changed. Also keep in mind the difficulties of second-guessing traffic patterns in San Francisco. My strong recommendation, although I know this one is hard, is not to schedule a romantic outing too tightly or you will be more assured of a headache then an affectionate interlude.

A few miscellaneous suggestions: Do not discuss money, family or the kids, keep your eyes on what's on your plate, not on his or hers; if you have a headache, take some aspirin now and not later; and regardless of how good-looking the person at the next table is, remember that distractions are never considered to be in romantic good taste. How different factors might affect your lips, not to mention your mood, is something to agree on before you head out the door, not after — or during.

In spite of all that, it is important to remember that part of the whole experience of an intimate time together is to allow whatever happens to be an opportunity to let affection reign. Regardless of what takes place, that is what is romantic. For example, remember the incredibly intense scene in the film *Body Heat*, where Kathleen Turner is standing in the hall and William Hurt smashes through the door (even though it appears to be unlocked) and rushes into her waiting arms, tumbling them both to the floor? Well, how romantic would it have been if Kathleen had started fretting about having to clean up the broken glass, get the door fixed and repair her torn underwear? Or remember the scene between Kevin Kostner and Susan Sarandon in *Bull Durham,* where he throws his full cereal bowl against the wall, cleans the kitchen table with a sweep of his arm and then picks Susan up and throws her passionately on the table? Well, how romantic would that have been if Kevin had started complaining about the broken china in his hair and the spilled milk running down his arms? Get the idea?

So, if the car breaks down, the waiter is rude to you, your reservations get screwed up, or both of you tire out and want to call it a day, you can still be endearing and charming. It really only takes an attitude change to turn any dilemma into a delight.

> "IN LITERATURE AS IN LOVE, WE ARE ASTONISHED
> AT WHAT IS CHOSEN BY OTHERS."
>
> *André Maurois*

◆ Bed & Breakfast/Hotel Kissing ◆

ARCHBISHOP MANSION

1000 Fulton Street, *at Fulton and Steiner*
(415) 563-7872
Expensive to Unbelievably Expensive

The lip ratings in this book indicate the amorous potential of a place based on a four-kiss system, but I would change my system just to grant at least 10 kisses to the opulent, self-indulgent style of living bestowed here. The outside world will melt into oblivion once you enter this august mansion turned bed & breakfast. As you cross the threshold it will be obvious what makes the Archbishop so magnificent. The massive foyer, a floral-patterned, handpainted ceiling in the parlor, the stained glass dome crowning the formidable three-story staircase, and Noël Coward's grand piano in the elaborate hallway are a few of the more notable appointments.

Each of the 15 lavish guest rooms are superbly designed for intimacy. In one, a claw-foot, white porcelain bathtub sits next to the fireplace. In another, the room's centerpiece is a four-poster bed from a French castle, placed in front of one of the 18 carved-mantel fireplaces that adorn the mansion. All of the rooms are decorated with choice antiques, embroidered linens, graceful sitting areas and a few even have city views. A gracious staff serves wine in the parlor and a generous continental breakfast comes to your door in the morning. The surroundings and the service at Archbishop Mansion allow guests to revel in the noble, gilt-edged style of the rich and famous.

♦ *Romantic Note:* Archbishop Mansion survived the 1906 earthquake — that alone should rate it a high kissing score.

♦ *Romantic Suggestion:* Take time to enjoy the quiet tree-dotted **ALAMO SQUARE** across the street. This park crests high above the city and offers one of the most remarkable views of San Francisco. On a sunny day, it's a lovely spot for a picnic.

THE BED AND BREAKFAST INN
4 Charlton Court, *between Laguna and Buchanan*
(415) 921-9784
Inexpensive to Expensive

This bed & breakfast was the first of its type in San Francisco, and its age adds to the hobbit-like pampered snugness that greets you upon entering. In the truest sense of the word, this inn is a hideaway, even though it is located in an area where that would seem to be an almost impossible accomplishment. The multitude of cosmopolitan shopping and dining selections on Union Street are only steps away from the front door, yet it will still be a simple task for you to surrender the pace of that urban world for this cheerful escape into contentment. The building was once a carriage house for the neighborhood. There are 10 rooms, all surprisingly adorable and dignified, including a select few that open onto their own hidden rooftop garden. Once you're both tucked under your overstuffed down-comforter bed, you may take a fancy to your new surroundings and want to remain here for breakfast. If not, the garden or the Colonial-style library may be your choice for discussing what the rest of the day will bring.

♦ *Romantic Warning:* The less expensive rooms share baths.

♦ *Romantic Suggestion:* Browsing hand in hand along **UNION STREET** is a one-of-a-kind elite shopping extravaganza. From the western edge of the Presidio to Telegraph Hill on the east, there is an endless procession of everything a curious consumer could want.

CAMPTON PLACE HOTEL — See Campton Place (Restaurant Kissing)

EDWARD II BED & BREAKFAST
3155 Scott Street, *on Scott at Lombard*
(415) 921-9776
Inexpensive to Moderate

This is one of my favorite bargain kissing places. The creative accommodations are bright, cheerful and beautifully renovated. Some of the rooms feature canopy beds, whirlpool baths and soft down comforters. The English country decor and wicker furniture in the common rooms create a summery feeling wherever you look. Breakfast in the morning is served at the inn's continental bakery next door. The lattes and fresh baked goods are some of the best in town. If the rooms weren't so affable, the bakery/coffee shop would be enough of a reason to find yourself stealing a kiss or two from the one you love here in the Marina District of San Francisco.

HERMITAGE HOUSE
2224 Sacramento Street, *between Laguna and Buchanan*
(415) 921-5515
Moderate to Unbelievably Expensive

This bed & breakfast is, when compared to others of its kind in the area, more traditional and definitely more subdued. Nonetheless, it is still romantic. So, when you think about distinctive places for a special night away together and you both want attentive service and luxurious surroundings, all those needs can be satisfied at Hermitage House. This four-story redwood mansion is a wonderful combination of formal sophistication and relaxed, country charm. The classic breakfast nook, the generous morning buffet, the grand fireplace in the library, the yellow brocade Queen Anne-period furnishings and the inviting, generous-size rooms all make for ardent accommodations. A visit here, if for only one night, will help you learn what being cozy is all about.

INN AT THE OPERA — See Act IV Lounge (Restaurant Kissing)

THE MANDARIN ORIENTAL HOTEL — See Silks (Restaurant Kissing)

THE MAJESTIC
1500 Sutter Street, *on Sutter at Gough*
(415) 441-1100
Moderate to Expensive

If ever you want a royal spoiling, The Majestic is the place to come. Several million dollars went into transforming this mansion into a designer masterpiece. A marble, mirrored entrance leads you to the imposing lobby area, where you will be greeted by a surprising mix of formality and friendliness. While the staff makes sure your room is perfectly prepared, you can appreciate the antique tapestries, etched glass and French Empire furnishings. You may even want to sip a cocktail at their authentic 19th-century mahogany bar. But don't linger too long; there is more waiting for you upstairs. The focal point of each room is a large, handpainted, four-poster canopied bed dressed in plump, feather pillows, fine linens and a plush down comforter. Radiating warmth from the fireplace offers even more enticement to lounge here like a king and queen, or prince and princess, or duke and duchess, or whatever you wish!

◆ *Romantic Extra:* **CAFE MAJESTIC,** (415) 776-6400 (Expensive) is considered by many to be one of the better restaurants in San Francisco. The stately dining rooms with their lofty ceilings and mirrors are done in shades of gray and peach. Even if you can't stay at The Majestic, try to make room in your plans for its fine food and elegant atmosphere.

THE MANSION HOTEL
2220 Sacramento Street, *between Laguna and Buchanan*
(415) 929-9444
Moderate to Expensive

The Mansion Hotel is a source of visual entertainment. The setting is a strange combination of flamboyant flourishes and fun. As you walk up the stairway to the entrance, a well-lit, fertile jungle motif lines your path. Prominent in the center of this tropical garden is a stone statue standing watch over this traditional San Francisco neighborhood. Once through the gothic doorway, the main floor is outfitted with a billiard room, a stage area where a magic show entertains on weekends, and finally, tucked around the corner, a thoroughly idyllic, crystal-chandeliered dining area. There are only a handful of tables arranged here in a glass alcove next to a floral garden dotted with Bufano sculptures. Both continental breakfast and dinner are served in this unique setting. It will be impossible not to give in to the obvious enchantment that accompanies your meal. All of the rooms are graced by a crystal decanter of sherry next to a queen-size bed, and a marble fireplace or a private terrace. The Mansion Hotel is a comfortable, playful palace that the two of you can rule over together.

MILLEFIORI INN — See Telegraph Hill (Outdoor Kissing)

PETITE AUBERGE
863 Bush Street, *between Mason and Taylor*
(415) 928-6000
Moderate to Expensive

The Petite Auberge has an attractive mixture of the winsome pleasures of a bed & breakfast and the courtly service and practicality of a downtown hotel. In the hub of San Francisco, this place showcases both those worlds. Whether you choose a room with or without a fireplace, you are still assured of an ideal, cheerful place to stay. That kind of guarantee can occur only when city life is replaced with the gracious charm of a French country inn.

Beyond the amiable accommodations, the continental dining service of this inn is first-class. The kitchen prepares a thoughtful breakfast buffet or a late afternoon sampling of hors d'oeuvres followed by a glass of wine. The dining tables are situated adjacent to a small garden, or you can choose to sit on loveseats next to a roaring fireplace. Either choice will tempt you to linger a moment or two longer to contemplate your upcoming schedule of events.

♦ *Romantic Suggestion:* The **FRENCH ROOM,** 495 Geary Street, (415) 775-4700 (Expensive) is probably one of the prettiest dining rooms in San Francisco. The provocative setting is adorned with stunning chandeliers, attractive seating arrangements and rich wood paneling. The food is consistently good and the atmosphere unceasingly heartwarming.

THE QUEEN ANNE
1590 Sutter Street, *on Sutter at Octavia*
(415) 441-2828
Moderate

As I stepped into The Queen Anne, I felt as if I had stepped into a different era where a kiss would make you blush and then long for more. The century-old ambience begins in the antique-adorned foyer where guests share tea or sherry by a blazing fire. The bottom of the cedar staircase is an impressive architectural centerpiece that rises four flights. Morning sunlight streams through the banister from stained glass windows and skylights. All of the 49 rooms are uniquely decorated with handsome English antiques. Your suite may have a curved bay window, a marble-topped dresser, a bathtub with claw feet, or a woodburning fireplace. Regardless of the mixture, each has its own grandeur to be cherished behind closed doors. After a restful night, fresh juice, croissants, coffee and a newspaper are served to you in your room.

◆ *Romantic Suggestion:* The Queen Anne is located in one of San Francisco's most colorful Victorian neighborhoods. Don't miss this opportunity to stroll arm-in-arm down the tree-lined streets and take in some of the architectural sights only this city can offer.

THE SPRECKELS MANSION
737 Buena Vista West
(415) 861-3008
Moderate to Expensive

Located on Buena Vista Hill just east of Golden Gate Park. Take Frederick Street to Buena Vista West and turn up the hill. The Mansion is across from the park and to your right. Twenty minutes from downtown.

Everything at the The Spreckels Mansion is so near perfect that the only reason not to plan a stay is the knowledge that leaving and returning home will be more difficult than most hearts could tolerate. Imagine rooms replete with Corinthian columns, canopied beds, some with bathtubs situated in front of glowing fireplaces, stained glass windows, sunrooms or sitting rooms — all within one immense, handsomely furnished home. Situated atop Buena Vista Hill, this residence is encircled by a neighborhood full of architectural pleasures. The street leading to The Mansion curves up and around Buena Vista Park, with flawless lawns, thickly arrayed arbors and manicured shrubbery. After a full day of delving into city life, you'll cherish these rare creature comforts.

WHITE SWAN INN
845 Bush Street, *between Mason and Taylor*
(415) 775-1755
Expensive

If I didn't write travel books I would definitely keep White Swan Inn as my own romantic secret. One of the risks of my profession is that in sharing the names of extraordinary places, I might have trouble obtaining a reservation for myself the next time I'm in town. Ah, what one must sacrifice for her craft!

White Swan Inn brings the English countryside to life in the heart of downtown San Francisco. The rooms are masterfully done, each with its own fireplace, stately antiques, floral bouquets and bay windows. As wonderful as the rooms are, you will enjoy sharing high tea (served every afternoon) in the courtyard garden or lingering over the bountiful breakfast served in the inn's intimate dining room.

◆ *Romantic Alternative:* **THE INN AT UNION SQUARE,** 440 Post Street, (415) 397-3510 (Moderate to Expensive). The lasting impression of your stay here will be one of cozy comfort, first-class style and dedicated service. All the rooms are outfitted with sitting areas, Georgian furnishings, lively fabrics and king-size beds. Each of the 6 floors has its own tranquil lounge with a crackling fireplace where afternoon tea or morning breakfast can be warmly savored. There is a grand suite on the top floor that has its own sauna, whirlpool bath, fireplace and bar. If you can't find romance here, you aren't likely to find it anywhere.

"LOVE, WITH VERY YOUNG PEOPLE, IS A
HEARTLESS BUSINESS. WE DRINK AT THAT AGE FROM
THIRST, OR TO GET DRUNK; IT IS ONLY LATER
IN LIFE THAT WE OCCUPY OURSELVES WITH THE
INDIVIDUALITY OF THE WINE."

Isak Dinesen

◆ Restaurant Kissing ◆

THE ACT IV LOUNGE and THE INN AT THE OPERA
333 Fulton Street, *between Gough and Franklin*
(415) 863-8400
Toll Free (800) 325-2708
Moderate to Very Expensive

When I first walked into The Inn at the Opera it was at the end of a long day. The way I felt, the Taj Mahal would not have impressed me. But from the moment I headed down the entry hall to the inn's restaurant, my mood made a 180-degree turn for the better. I was still exhausted, but I had found another kissing place. *Ah, sweet success!*

The Inn at the Opera offers a softly stated environment in which you will be spoiled more elegantly than at almost any other place you're apt to stay within the Bay Area. Inviting, overstuffed pillows and comforters, chocolates at bedside, and terrycloth robes all await you in a room subtly designed for provocative moments. And outside your front door is San Francisco's theatrical, artistic and political essence gathered in the cathedral-like buildings of the Civic Center. The highlight of your stay will be to discover The Act IV Lounge. This is a bastion of refinement and gourmet cuisine. The interior's handsome character is accented by a marble fireplace, mahogany pillars and muted lighting that gently illuminates the walls and furnishings. Seated at one of the handful of tables nestled about the room, you and your companion will be perfectly situated to enjoy the delights of the ensuing meal, from appetizer to final after-dinner drink — all to your hearts' content.

BIX
56 Gold Street, *between Pacific and Jackson*
(415) 433-6300
Moderate

An intimate evening doesn't always have to be discreet, cultivated and cosmopolitan — especially if you find yourselves as fully enamored of this vivacious, energetic restaurant as we did. Bix is certainly not the place to go if you want to whisper sweet nothings in each other's ears. But if you're looking for an incredible dinner and great entertainment, you'll love this place. Bix is really a supper club in the tradition of that now-rare genre of dining spots. While you're partaking of well-prepared dishes sprinkled with a few unusual ingredients the chef creatively tosses in, you might hear a torch singer or a saxophone player. Jazz is the theme here, and it shows in the mood and decor. The restaurant has two floors connected by a large staircase. Booths line the walls, and tables occupy the rest of the downstairs dining area.

CAFE MAJESTIC — See The Majestic (Hotel Kissing)

CAFE MOZART
708 Bush Street, *between Powell and Mason*
(415) 391-8480
Expensive

Thick red velvet and embroidered lace hang in the windows. Outside, people walk by and cars pass back and forth, but once inside you never take any notice of it. Cafe Mozart is probably one of the most intimate restaurants in San Francisco. There are just 10 tables here, each draped in white linen and set with fine china, silver, crystal and a single red rose. Around them, antiques, artwork and music by the real Mozart enriches the interior. The French cuisine is flavorful and beautifully presented. This is a very romantic place for a special occasion, even if the occasion is simply that the two of you are together.

CAFE POTPOURRI
905 California Street, *between Mason and Powell*
(415) 989-3500
Inexpensive

I am always in search of wonderful restaurants that specialize in breakfast and cafe au lait (or latte, depending on what country's cuisine or atmosphere you prefer). The Northwest, more than any other region in the United States, takes great pride in its coffee integrity. This stimulating morning ritual is not to be taken lightly. What better way to start the day than with ardent clinging and a steaming cup of espresso? Only a bona fide San Franciscan couple would understand what I'm referring to. Now, whether or not you buy any of this coffee romance, Cafe Potpourri is still an elegant place for your morning repast. Exquisite French pastries, interesting egg dishes and, of course, a precisely made cafe au lait are always available, and the kissing is up to you.

CAMPTON PLACE DINING ROOM
340 Stockton Street, *on Stockton at Sutter*
(415) 781-5155
Expensive

Campton Place is one of the most formal and praised dining experiences in San Francisco. Its elegance and refinement are actually quite dazzling. I would think twice about dropping your fork or napkin at this establishment (better to kick it under the table next to yours than admit to your own faux pas). Well, perhaps I'm exaggerating just a bit. This exceptional culinary landmark is where the elite come for very serious dining and very serious, very intense romancing. The American cuisine is sublime and, as you would expect, rather costly.

◆ *Romantic Suggestion:* Campton Place is open for a regal morning repast, with the same dazzling setting and service. It is less stuffy during the early morning hours. You could drop your napkin twice and no one would blink an eye.

◆ *Second Romantic Suggestion:* For the same intense style in accommodations, consider splurging by making reservations at the very posh, very deluxe **CAMPTON PLACE HOTEL**, (415) 781-5555 (Very Expensive to Unbelievably Expensive). Imagine a valet service that unpacks your baggage, brings fresh flower bouquets to your room, and provides shoeshining service. There are also plush carpets and handsome antique furnishings in every room. One wouldn't call Campton Place Hotel cozy; the only word for this place is aristocratic.

THE CLIFF HOUSE
1090 Point Lobos Avenue
(415) 386-3330
Moderate

Take Geary all the way to the ocean, where it dead-ends at The Cliff House.

All right, I know this is a tourist attraction. It would be hard to ignore the busloads of tourists that arrive here almost hourly to take in the stunning view of this landmark location. But note that word *"almost."* Late afternoon or early evening and the place may be practically empty. It is worth the risk, though, because The Cliff House offers an unparalleled view of the forceful, roaring ocean and the prolific sealife on Seal Rock below — a feast for the soul and eyes. The weather conditions won't affect anything adversely either. Whether the sun is sizzling onto the sea or you arrive on a fog-shrouded day, the waves colliding against the jagged black rocks at the base of the restaurant will compose a rhapsody you can call your own.

◆ *Romantic Note:* By the way, even the food is good. The Sunday buffet brunch in particular is a good idea if you go early enough or don't mind waiting.

DONATELLO

501 Post Street, *between Taylor and Mason*
(415) 441-7182
Very Expensive

The Italian Renaissance seems to be alive and well and thriving in glittering, noble style at Donatello's. Superior in every respect, this striking dining room with its stately decor and subdued lighting lends itself to a sensual evening of culinary delights. The food is remarkable and the presentations artful. The only other place you are likely to find meals prepared as expertly as this would be in Northern Italy. Thank goodness, Donatello's is in San Francisco, because dining here will make you feel like *Romeo and Juliet* with a happy ending.

◆ *Romantic Alternative:* There are several **UMBERTO RES-TAURANTS** in the world, but this one at 141 Steuart Street, (415) 543-8021 (Expensive) happens to be the most beautiful. Reminiscent of an Italian villa on a hill overlooking the Mediterranean, this is a lofty setting for a pasta extravaganza. Arched doorways, terra-cotta-tiled floors, provocative artwork and soft lighting create an eye-catching environment for conversation and *amore*.

THE FRENCH ROOM — See Petite Auberge (Hotel Kissing)

LE CASTEL
3235 Sacramento Street, *on Sacramento near Masonic*
(415) 921-7115
Expensive

   Located in a renovated home in the very fashionable Presidio
Heights neighborhood, Le Castel is a lovely place to dine on some
incredible French food and romantic atmosphere. This place offers a
welcome change of pace and temperament from the Nob Hill crowd.
That doesn't mean this isn't a thoroughly chic, posh dining experience, but the words ultra-chic and ultra-posh don't apply. Don't
forget to share a dessert or two; these are some of the most sinful
ones in town.
   ◆ *Romantic Alternative:* **CHEZ MICHEL,** 804 North Point
Street, (415) 771-6077 (Expensive) has an ambience that is lovely
and seductive. The interior holds a simple array of tables, shuttered
windows, Renaissance-style tapestries draped from the ceiling, brass
railings and long-stem candles atop each table. The food is superior
in every respect, in spite of the location. (The theory is that the
closer a restaurant is to Fisherman's Wharf, the further away it is
from serving a decent meal.) There are wonderful things happening
here: One of them is food, the other will be you two once you arrive.

THE MAGIC FLUTE
3673 Sacramento Street, *between Spruce and Locust*
(415) 922-1225
Inexpensive to Moderate

   This restaurant is a refreshing contrast to the affected style of many
formidable, highbrow dining establishments where you sense that if
you were to drop your napkin or fork, a waiter might reprimand you.
"Magic Flute" is a wonderful name for this angelic place. The blue
walls covered with a white trellis-like pattern, white filigree chandeliers and simple country tables and chairs create a light and airy
setting. Your sentiments will easily blend with this engaging atmo-

sphere as the evening slowly unfolds toward dessert. It would be an error not to mention the dedication this restaurant has to serving health-aware meals chosen from a diverse group of international cuisines.

LAS MAÑANITAS
850 Montgomery Street, *between Jackson and Pacific*
(415) 434-2088
Inexpensive to Moderate

Las mañanitas means "the early dawn." In Mexico City, it's the time of day a gentleman serenades his sweetheart on her birthday. At Las Mañanitas, during the early evening hours, you will be serenaded in kind by a strolling guitarist. It's just part of the festive atmosphere and Latin flavor of this appealing restaurant. On weekends after nine, the dining room heats up with live salsa music. Couples can keep rhythm at their tables, and the more adventurous can show off their rhythm on the small dance floor next to the fountain.

◆ *Romantic Note:* Las Mañanitas is built around a pretty patio and on warm afternoons you can enjoy lunch outside.

THE PEACOCK
2800 Van Ness Avenue, *between Lombard and Chestnut*
(415) 928-7001
Expensive

The Peacock restaurant is an ethnic culinary treat in a surprisingly posh Victorian setting of overstuffed chairs, supple floor-length curtains, intimate, cloistered dining rooms and graceful attentive service. If the two of you love East Indian cuisine, then this place is a rare find for a special private occasion. Their tandoori and vegetarian dishes are some of the best we've ever tasted.

◆ *Romantic Alternative:* **GAYLORDS**, 900 North Point Street,

Ghirardelli Square, Fisherman's Wharf, (415) 771-8822 is an impressive setting for excellent East Indian food. The ornate interior and attentive service are highlighted by huge bay windows that overlook the harbor and wharf below. The view is what lends magic to Gaylord's, and when an affectionate evening is at stake, a dramatic stroke may be what's required. Perhaps it's a bit too touristy to be considered totally romantic, but all the right ingredients are here for an intimate dining experience.

SILKS

222 Sansome Street, *between Pine and California*
(415) 986-2020
Moderate to Expensive

To arrive at Silks, you pass through the Mandarin Oriental Hotel's lovely lobby and ascend an elegant sweeping staircase. The center-piece of this dining room is a splendid copper-and-brass table plumed with a profuse floral bouquet and a copious amount of fruit, breads and liqueurs. Encircling this display are tables set well enough apart to provide each with a considerable amount of proper intimacy. The food at Silks is imaginative, combining French tradition with oriental ingredients and the zest of California cooking. As its name suggests, Silks has a soft atmosphere that makes it a comforting place for tender time together.

◆ *Romantic Option:* **THE MANDARIN ORIENTAL HOTEL,** 222 Sansome Street, (415) 885-0999 (Unbelievably Expensive) is an outstanding, albeit business-oriented, place to stay while you are in San Francisco. The guest rooms are located on the top 11 floors of the 48-floor twin towers of the California Center. Every room has an unbelievable view, and some have marble bathtubs with the same celestial perspective of the city.

SHADOWS RESTAURANT — See Telegraph Hill (Outdoor Kissing)

TOMMY TOY'S
655 Montgomery Street, *between Washington and Clay*
(415) 397-4888
Moderate

There are no chopsticks at this ambrosial location. That's because Tommy Toy's is different: It's Chinese cuisine with a French flair. There aren't many restaurants I know of where you can find Peking duck served with crepes for the main course, and a fluffy, smooth chocolate mousse for dessert. Elaborate is the only word to adequately describe the decor. The restaurant is patterned after the 19th-century Dowager Empress's reading room, and she obviously knew how to live. These ornate surroundings are subdued by candlelight and fresh, fragrant flowers. If you're just looking for a good Chinese dinner, you'd do best to go elsewhere. Here at Tommy Toy's you will find a unique dining experience that should be shared with your special someone.

"IN THEIR CHOICE OF LOVERS, BOTH THE MALE
AND FEMALE REVEAL THEIR ESSENTIAL NATURE.
THE TYPE OF HUMAN BEING WHICH WE PREFER
REVEALS THE CONTOURS OF OUR HEART."

José Ortega y Gasset

◆ Cabaret/Lounge Kissing ◆

THE CARNELIAN ROOM BAR
555 California Street, *in the Bank of America building*
(415) 433-7500
Very Expensive

Fifty-two floors above it all, the glass-enclosed lounge at The Carnelian Room offers a mesmerizing view of San Francisco. It is one of the unrivaled high points of the city. For this stellar experience, you will want to arrive just before sunset. The last light of day will cast striking shadows across the city. Lights from the buildings at first shimmer in the dusk, and later, sparkle brilliantly against the black velvet sky. All this heavenly grandeur serves as a poignant backdrop to the posh interior, which fits two very nicely.

◆ *Romantic Warning:* The Carnelian Room restaurant is reputed to serve an overpriced, mediocre dinner. On Sunday, however, an expensive though decent brunch is served, with the same view as from the bar.

◆ *Romantic Option:* You'll find another scintillating view of San Francisco at **VICTOR'S**, 335 Powell Street, (415) 397-7000 (Very Expensive). An outside, glass-walled elevator takes you to the restaurant on the top floor of the Westin St. Francis Hotel. Here, floor-to-ceiling windows disclose what sitting on Cloud Nine is really like. The continental cuisine is excellent and the service superior. If there is any drawback, it's popularity and tourists, but watch the view and you'll only see the city and each other.

PIAZZA LOUNGE
55 Cyril Magnin Street, *in the Park 55 Hotel*
(415) 392-8000

The competition among large downtown hotels in San Francisco is apparent in their progressively more elaborate interiors, ranging from futuristic to flashy to opulent. The intention, of course, is to impress the business traveler or out-of-towner with the hotel's image and design. From the older hotels with their baroque, florid interiors, to the prodigious, ultramodern design of the newer hotels, impressive isn't exactly the word — exaggerated is probably more applicable. All this can indeed be fascinating, but having a meal or drink in that kind of setting is more like touring a museum than relaxing in a romantic respite.

Perhaps one of the few exceptions is the cocktail lounge at Park 55 Hotel. It ingeniously unites conspicuous, contemporary extravagance with beautiful, intimate comfort. At Piazza Lounge, the evening can be initiated with a heart-to-heart discourse on the evening's possibilities. Sink back into a billowy chair as the sounds of the grand piano drift about the room. The intriguing artwork and the crystal chandeliers that dangle from the four-story ceiling will help give your evening or afternoon a sultry start.

THE PLUSH ROOM
940 Sutter Street, *between Hyde and Leavenworth*
(415) 885-6800
Expensive

Remember those late-night movies in black and white from the '40s where hearts were lost, found, broken and mended all at a quiet table in the corner of a jazz club? There was always moving music in the background that would reach a crescendo just in time for the lovers to join in a torrid embrace. The Plush Room keeps alive this tradition of steamy jazz and soothing contemporary ballads in an appropriately classy, intimate setting. Whether or not you are a jazz connoisseur, you'll find this place a tempting spot to share with your partner. You may be surprised to discover that words will be of no practical use all evening long.

THE VENETIAN ROOM

950 Mason Street, *between Sacramento and California*
(415) 772-5163
Very Expensive

An exceedingly amorous way to take a two-step into the past is to go dancing at The Venetian Room. Their 10-piece orchestra plays melodies that can coax even the most reluctant onto the dance floor for a little cheek-to-cheek foxtrot. This must be the way it was back in the '30s or '40s when a night out on the town meant dinner and dancing (not dinner and disco). The tiers of tables surrounding the dance floor create intimate montages throughout the room. After you've tripped the light fantastic, headline entertainers do their thing. On any given night, that could include someone like Ella Fitzgerald or Sarah Vaughan serenading you with their enduring vocal talents.

◆ ***Romantic Alternative:*** If the steep cover charge of The Venetian Room seems prohibitive, try the somewhat more reasonably priced musical rhythms of the **NEW ORLEANS ROOM**, in the Fairmont Hotel, (415) 772-5259. This is swing at its best, with all the smoothness and intoxicating renditions that will make you sway and move to the beat like never before.

> "BEAUTY IS HOW YOU FEEL INSIDE,
> AND IT REFLECTS IN YOUR EYES. IT IS NOT SOMETHING
> PHYSICAL OR UNDERSTOOD BY ANYONE ELSE
> BUT YOUR BELOVED."
>
> *Sophia Loren*

◆ Outdoor Kissing ◆

ALAMO SQUARE — See Archbishop Mansion (Hotel Kissing)

GOLDEN GATE BRIDGE

Lincoln Boulevard, Park Presidio Boulevard and Lombard Street all merge onto the Golden Gate Bridge. There is a parking area just east of the toll booths. From here you gain entrance to the walkway across the bridge.

Walking over the venerable, symbolically stoic Golden Gate Bridge is an exhilarating, unforgettable journey. This monumental structure offers views that can only be described as astonishing. From this vantage point you can survey the city's physique while you soar high above it, unencumbered by buildings or earth. The Pacific Ocean, 260 feet below, is an endless blue apparition framed by the rugged curve of land north to Marin and south to San Francisco. As unbelievable as it sounds, the gusts of wind up here can cause the reinforced, herculean lines of steel cables to sway effortlessly to and fro. This is the time and place where, without even kissing or touching, you can really feel the earth move — and it won't be from an earthquake either. On a clear, sunny day, just once in your life, put on your walking shoes and discover this one for yourselves.

◆ *Romantic Option:* **GOLDEN GATE PROMENADE** wraps 3½ miles around one of the most astounding scenic routes the Bay Area has to offer. This walkway extends from **AQUATIC PARK** at Fisherman's Wharf to **FORT POINT** under the protection of the Golden Gate Bridge. If there is a lover's lane to be found anywhere in San Francisco it would be the projection of land at Fort Point. As you gaze out to the golden rocky hills, the vast lengths of the Golden Gate and Bay Bridges, the glistening blue water and formidable cityscape, there is little else to do but nuzzle close and kiss.

GOLDEN GATE PARK

Between Lincoln Way, Fulton Street, Stanyan Street and the Pacific Ocean.

For those who know this vast acreage of city woodland and gardens, it is possible to imagine that Golden Gate Park and Romance are themselves an adoring couple. There is so much to see in this diverse three-mile-long park that one day here and you will only scratch the surface. Nevertheless, once you begin to experience the park's varied sensations, you will assuredly have your prelude to an enchanting day together. You can start at the **STRYBING ARBORETUM**, a horticultural wonderland of plants and trees from all over the world. Another remarkable city escape is the **JAPANESE TEA GARDEN**. The exotic display of Japanese landscaping gives a tranquil reprieve from anything having to do with urban life. While school is in session, the **CHILDREN'S PLAYGROUND** with its extraordinary carousel offers adults a grand backdrop for playtime. The **CONSERVATORY OF FLOWERS** is a stunning structure that houses many of the earth's most brilliant colors and plantlife. Wherever you find yourselves, this magical San Francisco park is the foremost outdoor spot of the city.

PIER 39

At the foot of Beach Street at Embarcadero.

Okay, call me a kid, I won't be insulted. After all, it might be easier sometimes to see life through the eyes of a child. In the case of Pier 39, if you don't use a younger viewpoint all you're likely to see is a sizable tourist attraction. Try my approach and spend your time on the carousel eating cotton candy or riding the bumper cars. Or you can investigate the teddy bear store, home to over 2,000 of these huggable creatures. Or watch the mimes, magicians and musicians perform while you wrinkle your nose at the smell of the sea and squint at the sparkling reflection of the sun on the ocean. On a nice day, you're sure to see sailboats whipping across the water with the wind.

On the tourist side of things, more than 100 shops line the two-story boardwalk. There are at least a dozen eating spots for practically every taste and budget, and as an extra incentive many of the restaurants have views of the bay. At Pier 39, if you're willing to adjust your biases and be young-at-heart, this can be a pretty neat place practically any day.

◆ *Romantic Suggestion:* Take a cruise on the photogenic San Francisco Bay. **THE BLUE AND GOLD FLEET** (415) 781-7877 is docked at Pier 39's west marina. Scenic, very touristy tours depart frequently. You won't be alone, but if you concentrate on the scenery the crowds will be much less apparent.

TELEGRAPH HILL

From Union Street, head east up Telegraph Hill.

If you live in or visit San Francisco regularly, there is probably one place that symbolizes for you what this city is all about. For some it's Fisherman's Wharf, for others it's Union Square, for some eccentrics it may be Alcatraz. For a total, all-encompassing overview it would have to be either Twin Peaks or Telegraph Hill. For kissing, I nominate Telegraph Hill.

The top of Telegraph Hill is where the famous Coit Tower presides over the city. From this vantage point you get a sense of the city's passionate personality, its pulsating energy as well as its orderly, well-contained physique. You will also be exposed to a lot of other sightseers, which may obscure the view and reduce your hope for a romantic measure of time. But then again, when you actually witness the sights and sounds from this pinnacle, you may find that the crowds around you don't seem to matter. It's worth the risk!

◆ *Romantic Suggestion:* When you've finished admiring this hallowed view, be sure you have made dinner reservations at **THE SHADOWS RESTAURANT**, 1349 Montgomery, (415) 982-5536

(Expensive), which resides on the easternmost flank of the hill just
a stroll's length down from Coit Tower. Here the crowds will seem
to melt away as your emotions and tastebuds come alive. This pastel,
high-beamed restaurant overlooking the Bay has floor-to-ceiling
picture windows, high-backed wicker chairs, apricot-colored tablecloths, pine paneling and an open, airy atmosphere. As you relish
the Californian cuisine, you can watch the mosaic patterns of water
and sky alter as the day makes its transition into night.

◆ *Romantic Warning:* Depending on the time of day, you may
find yourselves waiting in a line of traffic while you make your ascent
to the top of Telegraph Hill.

◆ *Romantic Suggestion:* At the foot of Telegraph hill is the North
Beach area, overflowing with Italian restaurants and Italian bakeries
that tantalize the senses. In the midst of this ethnic paradise is the
MILLEFIORI INN, 444 Columbus Avenue, (415) 433-9111
(Moderate to Expensive) where you can feel connected to the unique
city life of San Francisco. This European-style bed & breakfast has
an artistic blend of chandeliers, rich wood paneling, stained glass
windows, polished brass and graceful antiques throughout each and
every room. Millefiori Inn is a unique alternative, not only because
of its location but because of its inviting personality and diligent
attention to service.

"COMPARED TO OTHER FEELINGS,
LOVE IS AN ELEMENTAL, COSMIC FORCE WEARING A
DISGUISE OF MEEKNESS... IT IS NOT A STATE OF MIND;
IT IS THE FOUNDATION OF THE UNIVERSE."

Boris Pasternak

SOUTH OF SAN FRANCISCO

PILLAR POINT INN, Princeton-by-the-Sea
380 Capistrano Road
(415) 728-7377
Moderate

Twenty five miles south of San Francisco, just off Highway 1. Turn off Highway 1 at the traffic light for Capistrano at Princeton-by-the-Sea. Then turn into the harbor down by the water. The inn will be on your right.

A short 25-mile journey south of San Francisco will place you at the front door of a seaside lodging where you can immerse yourselves in quiet, carefree time together. The 11-room inn is not quite a bed & breakfast, and it is not anything like a typical hotel either. Pillar Point Inn looks like a New England-style home. From every room you can sit back and evaluate the profile of the harbor, ocean and coastline. At your leisure you can review all the movement in the harbor. The boats anchored close to shore will rock in rhythm with the waves, and the fishing boats will come and go with your increasing expectations of a fresh fish dinner. Accompanying this tableau are a fireplace, downy European feather bed, private steambath, and if you prefer, breakfast in bed. New England was never this warm or this close to San Francisco — till now, that is.

◆ *Romantic Note:* For a momentary change of pace from the solitude of Pillar Point Inn, be sure to stop across the street at **THE SHORE BIRD RESTAURANT**, 390 Capistrano Road, Princeton-by-the-Sea, (415) 728-5541 (Moderate). The outside closely resembles a Cape Cod cottage and is bedecked by cypress trees and a flower garden. Inside, the rustic furnishings and low ceilings are a friendly, easygoing accompaniment to the menu of locally caught fresh fish. Romancing may not be the primary reason to visit the Shore Bird, but the food and relaxed pace certainly are something you can get accustomed to.

CYPRESS INN, Miramar

407 Mirada Road
(415) 726-6002
Expensive to Very Expensive

From Highway 1 turn west on Medio and then north on Mirada.

This newly built contemporary structure sits on 5 miles of dreamy, white sand beaches. Every room is endowed with a seductive seaside view, fireplaces, private decks, and private Jacuzzi. The emphasis here is on beachside living, where a few steps from the front door is the boundless blue Pacific Ocean. Extended walks along the shore here will happily influence your feelings and desires. It will be hard to resist the effect this scenery can have on your lives. In the morning the breakfast is an unforgettable cornucopia of gourmet delights. At night, when you retire back to your lavish room, with the fireplace glowing against the darkness and the sound of the surf caressing the air, you will have a perfect prelude to a magical evening.

HALF MOON BAY

Take Highway 1 or Highway 280 south from San Francisco, and then Highway 92 into town.

When the rest of the world is heading north of San Francisco for Stinson Beach and other points along the exquisite Marin and Mendocino County coastlines, you can be winding your way a short, scenic drive south to Half Moon Bay. It is a quintessentially quaint little hamlet by the water that feels literally a hundred miles away from big-city life and, in comparison to its northern counterparts, is relatively unpopulated.

Half Moon Bay lovingly hugs the seaside along the rocky Pacific Coast Highway. It is replete with miles of sandy beaches, equestrian trails, bicycle paths, fishing charters, sailing sessions and whale expeditions. Combine all of that with the epic scenery and, believe me, it is difficult not to find a place that is suitable for hugging and kissing. There are also wineries, charming little lunch spots and plenty of parks to help round out your day. At night there are restaurants serving up an eclectic assortment of cuisines and prices, or clubs featuring classical and jazz music. Both can keep you busy well into the wee hours of morning, unless of course you can find something better to do.

MILL ROSE INN, Half Moon Bay
615 Mill Street
(415) 726-9794
Expensive to Very Expensive

Two blocks west of Main Street at the corner of Mill and Church.

From the moment we saw it, we knew Mill Rose Inn would be an affectionate place for a not-so-out-of-town sojourn. We entered through a classic white picket fence that wrapped around a slightly overgrown garden bursting with a beaming array of color. Sleeping in the sun, curled up lazily on the front porch, was the inn's cat, who conveyed the notion that here was a carefree, easy place. Here we could shake off our frazzled city nerves and find serenity and quiet.

There are 7 suites in this spacious home, and each is subtly and appreciably different. Two of my favorite rooms are the Briar Rose and the Bordeaux Rose. The snug and homey Briar Rose has a large bay window big enough for two, a handpainted tile fireplace and an ample bathtub (also big enough for two). The Bordeaux Rose is intimate and inviting. Shades of peach and ivory accent a lace-covered canopied bed framed by a handsculpted stained glass window. If you get tired of your room, which hardly seems possible, a flower-shielded gazebo encloses a Jacuzzi spa. Don't worry about finding a crowd in the spa — you can can reserve time here for a private, hot steamy soak of your own. After a good night's sleep, a champagne breakfast is served in the dining room, or if you prefer, the same can be delivered to your suite. I think that last option is definitely preferable.

OLD THYME INN, Half Moon Bay
779 Main Street
(415) 726-1616
Very Inexpensive to Moderate

Seven blocks south of Highway 92, on Main Street.

Sometimes "cute" can spark even the most skeptical among us to
expose our amorous, snuggly side; at other times it can do just the
opposite. The Old Thyme Inn is careful to make sure their cute
touches are only warmhearted, not trite or corny. The well-behaved
puppy looking up at me with eyes pleading for attention, and the
stuffed animals in every room captured my heart. This handsomely
renovated home, built in 1899, packed with a sense of history, also
felt warm and affable. The rooms are simple, but each has its own
private bath and each is outfitted with something distinctive that
makes it welcoming and provocative: a fireplace, a four-poster bed,
a whirlpool bath built for two or a stained glass window, to name a
few. In the evening, wine and sherry are served around a woodburning
stove in the parlor. Breakfast in the morning is always a feast,
garnished by clippings from the inn's overproductive herb garden
which contains over 80 aromatic varieties that are available for tasting
by guests with inquiring tastebuds. This may not be the most luxurious
place you'll ever stay, but it may be one of the more interesting.

SAN BENITO HOUSE RESTAURANT, Half Moon Bay
356 Main Street
(415) 726-3425
Very Inexpensive to Moderate

Three blocks south of Highway 92 at the corner of Main and Mill.

The aroma of freshly baked bread caught my attention as I happened
past the San Benito House Restaurant one extremely lazy, sun-

drenched summer afternoon. Unfortunately, it was not open for lunch that day. I continued on, but found nothing else particularly interesting. As the day progressed, that tempting bouquet lingered in my memory and I couldn't resist the idea of returning for dinner. We called for reservations and went that same evening.

This French country dining room is adorned with a fanciful blend of dried and fresh flowers, wicker baskets and original oil paintings. The lasting impression is one of charming sophistication. Guests who know the restaurant call first to see what the chef has prepared for dinner. The prix fixe meal consists of several courses and a choice of three entrees. Almost always, fresh fish brought in by local fishermen and fresh produce from local farmers are included. Our dinner that evening was delicious, the service professional and helpful, and the homemade bread tasted as good as I had hoped for.

◆ *Romantic Warning:* The hotel attached to San Benito House is not as expensive as some of the other places to stay in Half Moon Bay, but be definitely forewarned: It is not anywhere near as nice either.

BELLA VISTA, Woodside
13451 Skyline Boulevard
(415) 851-1229
Moderate to Expensive

From Highway 101 or Highway 280, take Highway 92 west to Skyline Boulevard, turn left and follow the road about 5 miles to the restaurant, which is on your left.

Bella Vista is rustic on the outside and perhaps a bit too formal on the inside, but an abundance of floor-to-ceiling windows helps to create an environment that blends refreshingly with the expansive wooded exterior. The view seems to go on and on, with a rolling procession of redwood trees ending with the blue outline of the bay. It is best to plan an evening here when you can take full advantage of all that this location has to offer. Arrive before sunset so you can have dinner while darkness begins to veil the area in velvety black. If you've timed things just right, dessert will be served as the lights of the towns below begin to twinkle in the distance.

LA FORET, San Jose
21747 Bertram Road
(408) 997-3458
Moderate to Expensive

From Highway 101 take the Capitol Expressway to the Almaden Expressway and head south until you reach Almaden Road. Turn right and watch for the La Foret sign on the left.

Just a short drive away from the high-tech world San Jose is famous for, La Foret is known to be one of the prettiest restaurants in the South Bay. Located in the historic village of New Almaden, the restaurant sits next to a brook in what was the first two-story adobe hotel in California. The original wood paneling still frames the sizable windows that look out onto the wooded landscape. The French food is very good and the service outstanding. Soft candlelight will cast a gentle glow on the interior as you lovingly share your evening together here.

SEBASTIAN'S, Campbell
1901 South Bascom Avenue
(408) 377-8600
Expensive

Located in the Pruneyard Towers on South Bascom Avenue near Hamilton.

I heard someone at a table next to ours say, *"I feel like I'm on top of the world."* Perhaps that was a bit exaggerated, but it did feel somewhat like that, 17 stories up at Sebastian's. This restaurant is in the tallest building between San Francisco and Los Angeles, and offers a remarkable, unobstructed view of Silicon Valley, which, from this vantage, actually looks beautiful. At night after the sun goes down and the city lights are sparkling below, it is a favorite dining spot for couples. The food is Mediterranean, and after dinner there is dancing upstairs in the lounge.

♦ *Romantic Option:* For a different dining experience in the town of Campbell, I highly recommend **CAMPBELL HOUSE,** 106 East Campbell Avenue, (408) 374-5757 (Moderate to Expensive). This cozy restaurant provides a homey atmosphere, attentive service and delicious food, all in just the right proportions. Located in a 60-year-old home adorned with a lovely fireplace, sun porch and only 12 very intimate tables, it is a pretty setting for a meal.

SARATOGA

From San Francisco head south on Interstate 280. Take the Sunnyvale-Saratoga Road exit south to Saratoga.

Our weekend in Saratoga began with a visually stirring yet relaxing drive on an early-spring Sunday morning. A typical foggy San Francisco sky accompanied us for about two-thirds of the way. In the distance we could see that sultry sunshine would greet our arrival.

Everything about Saratoga was picture-perfect — the surrounding forest and parkland, the tall shade trees lining residential streets where much pride seems to be taken in well-tended gardens and homes, and the Victorian storefronts in the tradition of country shopping. The main street, Big Basin Way, is at best described as petite, but we still had no trouble finding a fair number of award-winning restaurants that scored as high on the kissing-rating scale as they did on the culinary one. There's more then enough in Saratoga for a superlative afternoon or weekend interlude.

♦ *Romantic Warning:* Due to the growing popularity of the Paul Masson Concert season, there are times when Big Basin Way is a traffic bottleneck the likes of which are not supposed to happen

outside the city. At least not when I'm there. Keep your schedule
loose if you happen to be here at the end of a concert. Simply park
your car and have a snack or cappuccino at any of the dining spots
along Basin Way.

BELLA MIA, Saratoga
14503 Big Basin Way
(408) 741-5115
Inexpensive to Moderate

Two blocks west of Sunnyvale-Saratoga Road.

A gentle breeze swirls across the porch at Bella Mia, brushing our
cheeks with cooling relief from the intense sun overhead. The air
rustles the leaves that shade the table-clad deck where couples sit
and dine on designer cuisine — sipping steamy cups of espresso and
sharing decadent-looking desserts. This historic Victorian mansion
is beautifully renovated, which makes the atmosphere inside or out
notably romantic.

I would recommend the salmon ravioli with its ever-so-smooth and
creamy sauce, while my partner insists the lasagna he so stubbornly
refused to share is the best he ever had. After a few cajoling remarks
he eventually gave in and let me have a savory, cheesy taste. My
only regret after leaving Bella Mia was that I had not insisted on
having a few more additional nibbles of his lasagna. Out of regard
for the remainder of the evening, I restrained my interest in what
was on his plate and concentrated on him and the location we were
sharing.

HAKONE JAPANESE GARDEN, Saratoga
21000 Big Basin Way
(408) 867-3438

*Take Big Basin Way through town; about a mile up the road you will see
a turnoff sign on the left side of the street.*

We missed it the first time we visited Saratoga, but after several
friends who had been there before admonished us for not checking
out the Hakone Garden, we returned for what was supposed to be
an unbelievable outing. We searched valiantly for the turnoff sign.
Finally we saw it and followed it to one of the most serene settings
I've ever seen. It was a horticultural utopia, pure and simple and
sublime.

Righteous redwood trees stretched to the sky, sheltering a sculptured
landscape of exquisite flora and fauna. In the center of the garden is
a blue pond where white lily pads float effortlessly over the surface,
and sleepy carp, a Japanese symbol of love and longevity, languish
in the still water. A cascading waterfall rushes into the pond, filling
the air with a mild tranquilizing sound. The garden is edged with
wood-fenced walkways adorned by delicate, sweet-smelling flowers.
The contemplative mood of the area makes it prime territory for a
walk with the one you love.

♦ **Romantic Note:** Food is not allowed in the garden, so a picnic
is out. But if you truly want to experience the flavor of this exotic
place, authentic Japanese tea ceremonies are performed on weekends.
Reservations are required, so call ahead if you want to be served.

THE INN AT SARATOGA
20645 Fourth Street
(408) 867-5020
Expensive to Unbelievably Expensive

One block north of Big Basin Way on Fourth Street.

If the idea of a bed & breakfast strikes you as a little too casual or informal, The Inn at Saratoga is much slicker than that. Or if a hotel seems too cold and practical, this inn is much warmer than that. It has the best of what makes some hotels distinctive and most bed & breakfasts quaint and cozy. These are attractive, bright suites with all the amenities that seasoned travelers require and romantics yearn for. For the purposes of this book, one of the most appealing details here is the balcony that comes with each room. These private viewpoints face a small forest of sycamore, maple and eucalyptus trees, with a creek flowing through the center, butterflies breezing by and birds serenading with melodic songs. As you stand on your balcony watching the sunlight flirt through the branches and pinery, it is impossible not to feel the glory of a summer or autumn day. Imagine what a composed setting like this can do for those in need of heartfelt moments alone!

LA MÈRE MICHELLE, Saratoga
14467 Big Basin Way
(408) 867-5272
Moderate to Expensive

One block west of Sunnyvale-Saratoga Road on Big Basin Road.

When making reservations at La Mère Michelle, which you absolutely must do if you want to dine here, you will also have to make a delicate romantic choice: Do you want to eat indoors or outdoors? Inside you will find a refined restaurant, highlighted by crystal chandeliers, fine art and mirrored walls. Outside is an entirely different atmosphere that is equally enticing. The wooden deck is encircled by a short brick wall blooming with periwinkle-blue flowers. Candles softly light the patio which is decorated with more blue-and-white accents. Whichever you choose, you won't be disappointed, because your appetite requirements will be handled very nicely. Whether you dine inside or out, the food will be wonderfully French, and the enchanting atmosphere will be right for an evening of conversation and looking deep into one another's eyes.

LE MOUTON NOIR, Saratoga
14560 Big Basin Way
(408) 867-7017
Moderate

On Big Basin Way between Fourth and Fifth.

Le Mouton Noir is anything but "the black sheep" of Saratoga's restaurant row. The pink-and-dusty-rose paisley decor and Laura Ashley prints give a light and airy country feel to this classic Victorian dining room. French-inspired California cuisine is served with care, and the food is delectable. Whether you have lunch here, with sunlight streaming through the many windows, or bask in the glow of a lovely candlelit dinner, Le Mouton Noir is a delightful discovery for two hearts desiring to feast on fine food and romance.

PAUL MASSON VINEYARDS, Saratoga
14831 Pierce Road at Highway 9
(408) 741-5181

From Big Basin Way turn left on Pierce Road and follow the signs to the main gate.

Swirling above the idyllic town of Saratoga, up a steep and winding country road, the Paul Masson Vineyards reach out over the hilltops on some of the most august, sundrenched earth in the entire South Bay. Everything here seems almost too picture-perfect. Graceful trees rustle in the soft, billowing breezes. Grapevines arc across the mountainside, disappearing from sight as the land curves to meet another hill and still another. The panoramic view is something to behold day or night. Perhaps the only flaw in this majestic setting is that the Paul Masson Vineyards are not open to the public except during special events. The winery presents a spectacular summer concert series featuring entertainers who appeal to almost every audience. One weekend you might listen to the soulful sounds of Ray Charles, the legendary jazz renditions of Ella Fitzgerald, the country influence of a star like Ricky Skaggs or the penetrating tones produced by the talented Kenny G. Regardless of what you choose to hear, there will be something miraculous about listening to music in the mountains with a clear sky and the sweeping countryside as the only backdrop.

◆ *Romantic Warning:* On a summer day, sitting in an unshaded spot can be a melting proposition. Try to find protected seats or bring a sun visor, sunglasses and towels. On the other hand, at night the mountain breezes can be cooler than you might think. An extra sweater might keep shivers at a minimum.

◆ *Romantic Suggestion:* **THE PLUMED HORSE**, 14555 Big Basin Way, (408) 867-4711 (Expensive) is a series of exquisite dining rooms, each with a personality all its own. One is outfitted with Victorian antiques and opulent, red velvet furniture, while another has weathered-wood walls encircled by stained glass windows. The food is fine French and rarely disappointing. There is even dancing in the Crazy Horse Saloon next door.

SANTA CRUZ

On the Pacific Ocean, just off Highway 1.

To my way of thinking, Santa Cruz exists in a time warp. Somewhere between 1968 and 1972 all the clocks stopped and were not ever reset. That's not entirely accurate, but you will understand what I am talking about once you arrive. For certain you will recognize the distinctive signs of youth in the air here. The beaches and boardwalk practically overflow with teenagers and college students, especially when school is out. For those with a predilection for something other then surfboards, The Beach Boys and cruising, there is another side to Santa Cruz that can be charming and beautiful. You can drive through the verdant countryside or towering redwood forests, or walk along the open glorious coastline and observe the seascape change from peaceful sandy beaches to turbulent, pounding surf. Or stroll through the musuems, oceanfront amusement park (with an old wooden roller coaster), wineries and restaurants that all combine to make Santa Cruz a popular summer beach resort. You can discover it for yourselves off-season and fall in love all over again at a slower pace. What's your hurry? After all, it's only 1968.

BABBLING BROOK INN, Santa Cruz
1025 Laurel Street
(408) 427-2437
Moderate

From Highway 1 head west on Laurel Street to the inn.

An acre of redwoods, pinery, flowered gardens, tumbling waterfalls, a graceful babbling brook and covered footbridges highlight this delightful bed & breakfast. The landscaping from every perspective is impeccable. Inside, a French country atmosphere is evident throughout the guest rooms and cottages. There are 12 units here, some with private entrances, private decks, fireplaces, Jacuzzi bathtubs and sturdy canopied beds. A short stroll away are the beach and the sparkling waters of the Pacific. In the early evening, after a long day of building sandcastles, you will find wine and cheese waiting for you. In the morning a generous country breakfast will give the day a good start.

◆ *Romantic Suggestion:* **SHADOWBROOK**, Capitola, 1750 Wharf Road, (408) 475-1511 (Moderate) is probably the most often recommended romantic restaurant in the Santa Cruz area. Access to the dining room, which is located on the banks of Soquel River, is gained via a winding footpath or little red cable car that creaks over its tracks to a stop by the bar. The food is usually quite good, especially if you order what's fresh.

◆ *Second Romantic Suggestion:* **GREENHOUSE**, Soquel, 5555 Soquel Drive, (408) 476-5613 (Inexpensive to Moderate) offers a garden setting for lunch or dinner. You can choose between dining in the atrium next to a glowing fireplace or on the wooden deck surrounded by knotty oak trees, or in the dining room of the original farmhouse. The only drawback to romance is the family atmosphere, but if you focus on the farm setting and each other, no one else will exist but the two of you.

CASABLANCA, Santa Cruz
101 Main Street
(408) 426-9063
Moderate

At the corner of Main and Beach in the heart of Santa Cruz.

If you're looking for a restaurant with a view, you need look no further. This renovated 1918 mansion is directly across the street from the beach, and the dining room's tall stately windows overlook this wonderful sight. You'll glimpse boats rocking on the bay and the surf rolling onto the shore. Just beyond, the wooden pier seems to change moods as the sun sets and the lamp posts begin to brighten the scene. The cuisine is classic continental steak and seafood dishes, and the interior setting is as fetching as the view outside. After an enjoyable meal, don't be surprised if the one you're with reaches for your hand and says something like, *"I think this is the beginning of a beautiful friendship."*

◆ *Romantic Note:* Attached to the restaurant is the **CASA-BLANCA MOTEL** (Moderate to Expensive). The rooms here are spacious and attractive, most with spectacular views of the water and boardwalk. If you look past the boardwalk and focus your attentions on the Pacific Ocean in all its endless blue glory, your stay will be more mellow and intimate.

◆ *Romantic Alternative:* **DARLING HOUSE**, 314 West Cliff Drive, (408) 458-1958 (Moderate to Expensive) resides on a cliff, standing guard over Monterey Bay. From the large porch in front of this Spanish-style estate, you can watch the sun beating down on the bright, blue bay and the surfers patiently waiting just offshore for the next big wave. Inside, the dark wood accents in the living room are highlighted by the beveled glass windows all around. One guest room faces the beach and is elegantly decorated. An art deco tile fireplace in the corner warms the room on chilly evenings. Other rooms at the inn are not as large and don't have the same view, but one has a Chinese canopied wedding bed and another is bathed by the prismatic sunrise every morning through beveled glass windows.

◆ *Second Romantic Alternative:* **CLIFF CREST**, 407 Cliff Street, (408) 427-2609 (Inexpensive) is a Victorian paradise in a renovated Queen Anne-style home. The most interesting feature of this house is the solarium where breakfast is served every morning. Surrounded on one side by six tall windows with a border of stained glass, you will be showered by multi-hued sunlight. The guest rooms are cozy, the common areas pretty and inviting and more than worth the price.

PACIFIC GROVE SHORELINE

*Take Highway 1 to Highway 68 heading west. Highway 68 becomes Forest
Avenue. Take it all the way to the ocean, where you will find the Pacific
Grove shoreline.*

For now the developers have left the oceanfront of Pacific Grove
alone, which for them might be a disappointment but for you is a
definite kissing advantage. While you are on the Monterey Peninsula,
allow enough time to encounter this lovely shoreline. Patiently
saunter arm-in-arm along Ocean View Boulevard, where the whisper
of saltwater gently sprays over you as the waves thunder against the
rocks at water's edge. Here you can watch the sea otters splashing in
the kelp beds, the pelicans perching in a sunny spot, and, if the time
of year is right, maybe a whale or two will swim by as they migrate
south for winter. If your walk takes you to **LOVER'S POINT PARK**,
at the southern tip of Monterey Bay, consider packing a picnic to
share in the shade of a tree or in the warmth of a gloriously sunny day.

THE CENTRELLA, Pacific Grove
612 Central Avenue
(408) 372-3372
Moderate to Expensive

*From Highway 68 take Forest Avenue to Central, turn left and continue
2 blocks to the inn.*

It is evening and the logs in the fireplace are just beginning to
burn. What's left of daylight still filters through the beveled glass
windows that line an entire wall of the parlor. Freshly baked cookies
and a carafe of cream sherry sit on an old oak table. We decided to
pour ourselves a glass of sherry and nibble on a cookie or two while
we went over the details of the fantastic places we saw that day. The
Centrella makes the end of the day as wonderful as the beginning.
This is a homey, secure place to come back to after a long, unhurried
afternoon of meandering through the streets of Monterey and Pacific

Grove. The guest rooms are equally cozy. Select touches like brass beds, skylights and a claw-foot bathtub can be found in each. A brick walkway, bordered by a garden of camellias and gardenias connects the inn to private cottages that boast fireplaces and attractive sitting areas.

In the morning, we stirred to the scent of freshly brewed coffee as the innkeepers set out a breakfast buffet. The cool, crisp air tempted us to pull the covers close for just a few more minutes. We succumbed to the temptation and decided to get a slightly later start on the day than originally planned. When we finally made our way down to breakfast, the coffee was still fresh-brewed and the baked goods still warm. After this, anyone would feel pampered enough to survive until the next special outing.

FANDANGO, Pacific Grove
223 17th Street
(408) 373-0588
Inexpensive to Moderate

Just south of Lighthouse on 17th Street.

This engaging Mediterranean-style restaurant is a potpourri of options. Flowers and sunshine engulf a festive patio where outdoor brunch is a gratifying repast. Indoors a crackling fire and just a few tables in each of the three front dining rooms provide a more intimate eating experience. If you step down a curved stone staircase, there is a wine cellar set up for special occasions. In the glass-domed terrace, the scent of mesquite from the open grill mingles with the sounds of laughter and creates an informal supper setting. There is only one thing more tricky than deciding where to eat here, and that is deciding what to eat. The food is flavorful and most of it is created from century-old family recipes. Once the tough decisions are out of the way, though (all decisions should be this tough), you really can sit back and unwind. After all, isn't that what this evening is all about?

FISH AND BASIL, Pacific Grove

105 Ocean View Boulevard
(408) 649-0707
Inexpensive to Moderate

On Ocean View Boulevard between Eardley and Dewey.

A meal at Fish and Basil will provide you with a Parisian adventure. The restaurant resembles an outdoor cafe on the Left Bank along the Rue Saint-Germain. The walls are painted with Impressionistic murals of an afternoon on the streets of Paris. The only thing that brings your thoughts back to the California coast is the stellar, ringside view of the Pacific Ocean from your table near the window. As you settle in for dinner, you won't be surprised that fish is the specialty which the chef diligently provides night after night, with finesse and care.

GREEN GABLES INN, Pacific Grove

104 Fifth Street
(408) 375-2095
Moderate to Expensive

At the corner of Ocean View Boulevard and Fifth.

From the street the exterior is striking; from the front gate the surroundings look like the introduction to a fairytale come to life; and from the moment you step inside this Queen Anne-style mansion, you'll know you are about to begin an enchanting experience. The inn, as its name suggests, is a multi-gabled structure with leaded glass windows that accord a dreamy view of Monterey Bay. The parlor is a collection of antiques where a brightly painted carousel horse sits behind a sofa, stained glass panels frame the fireplace, and freshly cut flowers are arranged about the room.

Halfway up the stairs that lead to some of the guest rooms, a pair of teddy bears keep company on a small wicker chair. The rooms are decorated in paisleys and floral prints. Some have sloped ceilings, others have bay windows, fireplaces and scintillating views of the water. Regardless of which corner is yours, all entreat you to indulge yourselves in this soothing setting. At first sight, the Green Gables Inn will capture your imagination, and before you leave it will certainly capture your hearts.

◆ *Romantic Warning:* Some of the rooms share bathrooms, which in the opinion of the authors is not conducive to uninterrupted kissing. Be sure to request the rooms that have private facilities, unless your ability to partake in uninterrupted smooching is contingent upon a lower-priced accommodation.

◆ *Romantic Alternative:* The Green Gables has a sister inn called **THE GOSBY HOUSE**, 643 Lighthouse, (408) 375-1287 (Inexpensive to Moderate). This lovely Victorian bed & breakfast has all the charm of its sibling, including fireplaces and down comforters in the guest rooms, a generous buffet breakfast and late afternoon high tea. In fact, the only thing that's missing is the ocean view.

OLD BATH HOUSE, Pacific Grove
620 Ocean View Boulevard
(408) 375-5196
Moderate to Expensive

At the edge of Lovers Point on Ocean View Boulevard.

The Old Bath House is a beautiful oceanside dining experience. The fact that it's located at **Lovers Point Park** makes it even more romantic. Waves roll up onto the rocks right below your table. After the sun ebbs into the sea, only city lights in the distance compete with the flickering flames of candles alight all over the restaurant. Little can compete with the intimacy this place sparks, except the food, which is a unique blend of French and Northern Italian cuisine. The desserts are created by the kitchen's own pastry chef and worth every sinfully rich calorie.

SEVEN GABLES INN, Pacific Grove
555 Ocean View Boulevard
(408) 372-4341
Expensive

At the corner of Ocean View and Fountain.

The Seven Gables Inn is a prodigious yellow mansion trimmed in white that sits on a rocky promontory in Pacific Grove. From every room you have dramatic views of the glistening ocean and coastal mountains. This grand old house is filled with an extensive collection of fine art and antiques. Tiffany glass windows, Persian carpets, 18th-century oil paintings and marble statues are just some of the collector's items that adorn the inn. The interior is formal and polished, yet it is still a place where you will feel at ease instantly. Each guest suite is an extraordinary private escape. Broad windows draped in lace make the rooms bright and sunny by day. At night the classic lighting fixtures give each room a soft, warm glow. It must be the elegance and warmth that draws so many honeymooners to the Seven Gables Inn. On most weekends you will find couples spending their wedding night here. And even if it's not your honeymoon, all that romance is sure to rub off!

♦ *Romantic Option:* Up the street a few blocks, at **THE MARTINE INN**, 255 Ocean View Boulevard, (408) 373-3388 (Moderate to Very Expensive) a hearty breakfast is served, with a spectacular view of the bay. This towering pink mansion (yes, it really is pink) resides on the cliffs overlooking Monterey Bay. The rooms here are spacious (bordering on huge), furnished with authentic antiques, handsome wood detailing, and some have fireplaces and views of the water. Obviously the person who designed this inn had romantic liaisons in mind.

17-MILE DRIVE

From Highway 1 take Highway 68 west to Sunset Drive, go west again to the Pacific Grove entrance gate. There is a $5.00 entry fee.

This drive is so awesome and resplendent that it will take you much longer to travel this unspoiled terrain than its 17-mile length suggests. That's because you will want to stop several times along the way to witness the infinite variations as ocean and land meet along the Monterey Peninsula. White, foamy waves wash up on black rocks, sending a spray of sea into the crisp, clean air. Almost as if they were signaled, seagulls cry out as unruffled pelicans regain their perch near the water's surface.

As you round one spiral of road, a crescent-shaped, sandy cove is a calm place to pause. Here sunlight shimmers on the vast Pacific, and in the distance a sailing vessel slowly makes its way across the horizon. Many other turns will reveal undulating sand dunes, violent frothing sea currents and abundant marinelife sanctuaries. On your journey you will encounter the stark beauty of a lone cypress clinging to the side of a cliff, swaying effortlessly in the wind. Up a hill, as you turn to the east, you enter a deeply wooded area that shelters the palatial homes and estates that bedeck this illustrious landscape. There will also be the occasional world-class golf course to spy upon, but unless watching the rich and famous is your idea of an intimate interlude, a few more turns ahead and the natural beauty of the peninsula will be yours again.

MONTEREY

Monterey was once a part of Mexico, and that heritage is reflected in its venerable adobe homes and the meticulously maintained parks bursting with flowers. Many of the surviving historical landmarks now house museums and you can almost touch the past as you stroll by them. The main signatures of this well-known romantic destination are the cypress forests, rolling hills and spectacular rugged coastline. Because of Monterey's position at the edge of the Pacific, it offers those who stop here some of the same nuances that a small (relatively small) waterfront town would supply; almost everything you'll want to see and do is within walking distance. There are intriguing restaurants and hotels that take full advantage of the almost year-round mild weather. Many places are blessed with bewitching views of the clear aqua bay and vivid blue sky. Of course, there are also the concomitant tourist attractions, such as Fisherman's Wharf, Cannery Row and the Monterey Bay Aquarium, which means Monterey can also be dreadfully crowded. Fortunately, that can easily be dealt with by allowing yourselves to concentrate on the stunning location and architecture.

◆ *Romantic Possibility:* Speaking of popular destinations, **CANNERY ROW** in Monterey is a bustling reminder of how the more things change the more they stay the same. This building complex once thrived on the business of catching and canning sardines. Now it is a series of shops and restaurants in the business of catching tourists. Why would you want to kiss here? Well, actually you probably *won't* want to kiss here. What you could do, though, is browse, laugh, hold hands, stroll and have a leisurely meal by the sparkling blue Carmel Bay. Cannery Row is not what you would call romantic, but it can be fun, and that's a good prelude to just about anything — including kissing — anytime.

◆ *Second Romantic Possibility:* At the end of Cannery Row, **MONTEREY BAY AQUARIUM** (408) 649-6466 is another of the city's tourist attractions, but this one presents a not-to-be-missed opportunity to view the marinelife that abounds below the water's surface. This aquarium is one of the world's largest and best, housed in an unbelievably realistic underwater setting.

◆ *Third Romantic Possibility:* **FISHERMAN'S WHARF**, much like Cannery Row, is a location worth visiting for an hour or two on a sunny afternoon. Actually, it's not the facility that makes it worthwhile, it's the oceanfront location. Ambling down the boardwalk, your senses tickled with the smell and taste of the swirling, salty ocean currents, you will pass souvenir shops, stands selling okay-to-mediocre seafood, and lots of restaurants boasting views of the bay. Be sure to stop in at **RAPPA'S**, Fisherman's Wharf #1, (408) 372-7562 (Inexpensive) at the end of the pier. From the moment you enter, you will feel that the restaurant is floating. From tables near the window you can watch pelicans and seagulls skim over the water as they rush to feed on the fish piled high by the fishermen returning with their daily catch.

CAFE KIEWELS, Monterey
100-A Heritage Harbor
(408) 372-6950
Inexpensive to Moderate

Heritage Harbor is located at the corner of Pacific and Scott.

Dusk — that lovely limbo between day and night — is a majestic event in Monterey. The water over Carmel Bay turns dark blue as sunset shadows cover the ocean in a blanket of darkness. A few late-returning boats, with their wind-filled sails, make their way back to the harbor while the last rays of light paint the horizon golden and the sun slips out of view into the sea. How we love early evening! And Cafe Kiewels may be the best place to go after you've indulged this love. Besides, at this hour most of the other tourists have either left for the day or won't be arriving until later. We were lucky enough to have this charming outdoor cafe almost to ourselves. The food was satisfying and we were happy because as the sunset ended we knew the night was just beginning.

HOTEL PACIFIC, Monterey
300 Pacific Street
(408) 373-5700
Expensive to Very Expensive

On Pacific one block south of Del Monte.

With so many bed & breakfasts and small inns to choose from on
the Monterey Peninsula, it's hard to believe anyone would want to
stay at a big hotel. Hard to believe until you see a handful of the
very chic, very lavish hotels that have been developed in this area.
Hotel Pacific is one of them, and it seems more like a retreat than
a traditional hotel. The approach to this genteel escape reveals a
flowing fountain at the entry, ring-necked doves serenading in the
lobby, courtyards trimmed with weathered, wooden furnishings, and
dense flowering vines lining the pathways and walls. Terra-cotta and
Sante Fe print fabrics accent the guest rooms where a woodburning
fireplace, a thick, cushy featherbed, a separate living area and private
patio or balcony overlooking the ocean all feel appropriately
luxurious. The hotel is located in the heart of historic Old Monterey,
close to all of the things you will want to see in this town. But don't
be surprised if you find yourselves staying in your suite more then
wandering outside into the out-of-towner milieu.

◆ *Romantic Alternative:* The **MONTEREY PLAZA HOTEL**,
400 Cannery Row, (408) 646-1700 (Expensive to Very Expensive)
is located in the heart of Cannery Row, which would be a romantic
problem if it weren't for what happens once you step inside the foyer.
As your eyes scan the polished, marble floor, the cozy lounge, the
balcony and then look beyond to the horizon, most of the way is
filled with ocean. The water is the focal point of Monterey Plaza
Hotel. Waves break underneath the building and the sound of the
surf swells through its chambers and corridors. Many of the rooms
and suites have views of the bay. If yours doesn't, be sure to return
to the hotel's main balcony in time for sunset. Later, dinner at the
hotel's restaurant, **DELFINO'S**, will be a pleasurable interlude. From

its windows you'll admire the shimmering moondance across the bay and the sparkle of city lights twinkling in the distance.

♦ *Second Romantic Alternative:* On a downtown street, **THE MONTEREY HOTEL**, 406 Alvarado Street, Monterey, (408) 375-3184 (Moderate to Expensive) is small enough to be charming yet large enough to offer all the amenities of a larger resort. Some of the rooms and suites have views of the harbor and bay. Be sure to ask for a description of the room you are booking; while all of them are handsomely furnished, some are too small for even the most intimate of couples.

THE OLD HOUSE, Monterey
500 Hartnell Street
(408) 373-3737
Expensive

At the corner of Hartnell and Madison.

This meticulously renovated restaurant was built back when Monterey was still a part of Mexico, and the exterior of bright salmon-colored adobe seems to bring that history alive. A wheelbarrow filled with flowers stands by the front door, and potted plants hang down from the second-story terrace. As you approach the restaurant, you might want to take a moment or two on the front lawn, where a kiss under one of the old cypress trees will be a perfect appetizer for your upcoming meal. When appetizers no longer suffice, step inside where several dining rooms, upstairs and down, are warmed by burnished fireplaces and the soft pastel decor is subtly lit by handmade chandeliers. The food, according to the owner, is Californian-French, but I think he's confused, because the servings are much larger than that description would imply. The Old House prepares substantial portions of fresh fish and wild game. When your cravings are satisfied, stop once again on the verandah outside, where a kiss in the darkness will be something more to savor.

SARDINE FACTORY, Monterey
701 Wave Street, *on Wave at Prescott*
(408) 373-3775
Expensive

The Sardine Factory has the reputation of being one of the more romantic dining spots in Monterey, and as wary as we are about places with that kind of reputation, we agree — this one is an illustrious choice. The centerpiece of the lounge where we waited for our table to be ready is a stunning 120-year-old handcarved bar. Friends had told us to request seating in the Conservatory, one of the restaurant's five dining rooms, and they were right. Covered by a glass dome and surrounded by a garden, this lovely room was a prime setting for inspirational conversation and loving thoughts. In addition to the atmosphere, the menu was also impressive. The fresh seafood was delicious and the desserts were among the best we've ever tasted.

◆ *Romantic Warning:* We waited in the lounge about 20 minutes for our table. Often glowing reputations also mean delays, even when you have reservations.

SPINDRIFT INN, Monterey
652 Cannery Row
(408) 646-8900
Expensive to Unbelievably Expensive

On Cannery Row between Hoffman and Prescott.

In the midst of Cannery Row, right on the ocean, the Spindrift Inn is an elegant, ultra-chic, architecturally beautiful place to stay. The setting makes it even more attractive. Waves roar up onto the rocks below, and the smell of saltwater in the air turns the aesthetic suites into a sanctuary for interpersonal introspection. On the ocean side, there are window seats in each room to nestle in while you feel the surf's magnetism vibrate in the air. Inside a crackling fire bathes the hardwood floors, Oriental carpets, canopied beds and down comforters in an amber glow. If it's a warm evening, only one irresistible option could tempt you away from all this newfound comfort: a stroll along the silvery moonlit beach. In the morning a continental breakfast awaits you at your door, and in the afternoon high tea is served on the inn's rooftop garden where there's a magnificent view of Monterey Bay.

♦ *Romantic Alternative:* Just a few steps from Cannery Row, you will find the **VICTORIAN INN**, 487 Foam Street, (408) 373-8000 (Moderate to Expensive). This inn combines the grace of the past with the sleekness of the present. Though the accommodations are probably a bit too modern for some tastes (there is a second phone in the bathroom), the rooms are filled with enough old-fashioned personality to make up for it. There are fresh pastries presented for breakfast, wine and cheese are served in the salon during the late afternoon, and a garden hot tub is available for a long steamy soak any time of day.

CARMEL

After spending a great deal of my time looking for kissing places, I take some amount of pride in knowing that I've been to (probably) all of the most romantic places that exist in Northern California. From that perspective, when I say no other place I've seen is quite as quaint or as charming as Carmel, I'm saying a lot. Much of that allure I attribute to what Carmel lacks, namely billboards, neon signs, tall buildings, parking meters and high heels. (There is actually a law on the books stating that it is *illegal* to wear high heels on the sidewalks!)

Carmel is home to some of the most colorful shops, interesting galleries, adorable inns and finest restaurants in the state. Since these are clustered in a very small area, discovering all of Carmel is an outstanding way to spend the day. A few blocks away from the center of town are enviable seaside homes, and white sandy beaches lie just in front of them proffering a more restful way to while away the hours. Without question, you will find yourselves captivated by the town's charm and flawless setting.

◆ **Romantic Note:** Part of Carmel's appeal is its small size; most of the establishments don't even have numbers on their doors. Therefore, most of the entries in this section of the book do not include formal addresses, only street junctions. Once you are in Carmel, these will be more than enough to find your destination.

◆ **Romantic Options:** The accommodations in Carmel, hands down, are some of the best places for affection and romance I have seen anywhere. There are almost too many to mention. A few of my favorite bed & breakfasts are as follows:

COBBLESTONE INN, Junipero and Eighth, (408) 625-5222 (Moderate to Expensive). The common rooms at the Cobblestone Inn are hardly what anyone would call common. You cross a cobblestone courtyard to enter the living room, where a lavish breakfast buffet and afternoon hors d'oeuvres are served in front of a massive stone fireplace. The guest rooms have the same romantic feel, and woodburning fireplaces keep the mood just right. This is reputed to be one of Carmel's best-run bed & breakfast establishments, and in this part of the world that's saying a lot.

SAN ANTONIO HOUSE, San Antonio and Seventh, (408) 624-4334 (Moderate to Expensive). There are four generous suites here, each with its own entrance, fireplace and comfortable, cozy antique furnshings. Helping round out this intimate place are the gardens and stone terraces, plus it's only one short block to the sun-clad beach.

VAGABOND'S HOUSE INN, Fourth and Delores, (408) 624-7738 (Inexpensive to Expensive). This English Tudor home is engulfed by oak trees rustling softly in the breeze. The rooms are ample, with fireplaces, a decanter of sherry beside the bed, and a view of the inn's verdant garden. This is a great place to call home for a few days of time alone.

ANTON AND MICHEL, Carmel
Mission between Ocean and Seventh
(408) 624-2406
Expensive

As we walked by Anton and Michel one evening, it was obvious that there was something extraordinary about this restaurant. Impressive oil paintings hung on pastel walls, long, slender, white columns separated one part of the dining room from another, and one entire wall of windows framed a patio that had a cascading water fountain at its center. Quickly we made reservations for the next night. The setting seemed to inspire intimate conversation and long loving looks at each other — that is, until the food arrived. We tried the house specialty, rack of lamb, and would recommend it to anyone. It's cooked to perfection and carved at your table. A little later, after turning our attention back to each other, we ordered a chocolate concoction that was sinfully rich and beautifully served. We look forward to sharing many more memorable evenings at this restaurant.

CARRIAGE HOUSE INN, Carmel
Junipero between Seventh and Eighth
(408) 625-2585
Expensive to Very Expensive

After a long, long day of travel, all I can usually think of is, *"Let me lie down somewhere, anywhere!"* We arrived at Carriage House Inn on one of those exasperating kind of days; all we wanted was a place to rest. Yet what greeted us was so much more that our energy and hearts swelled. This enchanting country inn reflects the romantic spirit Carmel is famous for. In our room, touches of blue accented the large, white-quilted brass bed, and an exposed beam ceiling towered over our heads. Without hesitation, and believe me we were tired, we put a few logs on the fire and cuddled up in the bay window and admired the pastoral view. Even though we could have taken advantage of all that Carmel had waiting right outside our door, we stayed inside most of the time appreciating the fireplace and our warm affection for each other.

◆ *Romantic Option:* **THE SUNDIAL LODGE**, Monte Verde at Seventh, Carmel, (408) 624-8578, (Moderate to Expensive) is a cordial, cozy place for those staying overnight in Carmel. The rooms are done in an assortment of French Country, wicker and Victorian. The red-brick courtyard, surrounded by multi-colored flowers, is a nurturing place to spend time outdoors on a sunny afternoon.

LA BOHEME, Carmel
Dolores and Seventh
(408) 624-7500
Moderate

La Boheme is a small cafe with a festive European rural theme. The cottage-like interior has brightly painted walls and a pastel blue ceiling with handpainted white fluffy clouds daubed here and there. Each table is covered by a floral print cloth and fresh flowers. Besides the amiable details of the interior, the creative chef serves a three-course prix-fixe meal that changes every night. The homemade desserts are delicious and worth lingering over with the one you love and two spoons. By the way, the diminutive size of the restaurant is such that you won't have to worry about sharing this place with too many other hungry diners.

◆ *Romantic Option:* If La Boheme is filled, you may want to head over to **PATISSERIE BOISSIERE**, Mission and Ocean, (408) 624-5008, (Inexpensive). This polished, choice French restaurant has an eclectic menu serving everything from quiche to extravagant fish dishes. If you don't have dinner, a cappuccino and one of their wickedly rich pastries would be wonderful too.

LA PLAYA HOTEL, Carmel
Camino Real and Eighth
(408) 624-6476
Moderate to Expensive

The sun is setting in Carmel-by-the-Sea and the azure blue sky is brushed with shades of pink and lilac. Two blocks away, the Pacific Ocean peers at you through pine and cypress trees, and the sound of the surf against the shore echoes in the distance. From somewhere overhead, every now and then, a seagull lets out a piercing, haunting cry that fades in the wind. Here you are at La Playa and it is dazzling. This place, in spite of its "hotel" appellation, is the place to stay if you long for a graceful setting that also has the luxury of a larger establishment.

La Playa's lobby is warmed by an enormous fireplace and decorated with handloomed area rugs and antiques. The guest rooms are filled with handcarved furnishings reflecting a Spanish influence, and some have incredible ocean views and fireplaces. Surrounding this handsome Mediterranean-style villa are neatly manicured lawns awash with flowers. There is even a heated pool encircled by lavender poppies swaying on their slender stems. If you believe sheer beauty can conjure up romantic rapport, you will find just that at La Playa.

◆ *Romantic Alternative:* **PINE INN**, Ocean and Lincoln, (408) 624-3851 (Inexpensive to Expensive) has a slow-burning fire in the hearth of the main lobby, beside which is a loveseat of rich, red velvet. It would be easy to lose track of time here, were it not for the grandfather clock in the corner striking each hour. Upstairs, some of the guest rooms have fireplaces and ocean views, and all have comfortable antique beds and choice Edwardian-style furnishings. The restaurant at the inn is a bit formal, but all of the meals are very good. Be sure to have breakfast or lunch in the restaurant's gazebo. On a sunny day, the domed glass ceiling rolls back to reveal a crystal clear blue sky. (The Pine Inn is located in the heart of Carmel, close to the beach, shopping and theater.)

♦ *Second Romantic Alternative:* **THE CYPRESS INN**, Lincoln and Seventh, (408) 624-3871 (Moderate to Expensive) is inspired by the same Spanish influence as La Playa Hotel, but it is a much smaller place. While the rooms here are not quite as elaborate, the simple beauty of the inn does evoke the appropriate frame of mind for encounters of the heart.

♦ *Romantic Suggestion:* The **THUNDERBIRD BOOKSHOP AND RESTAURANT**, 3600 The Barnyard, (408) 624-9414 (Inexpensive) is not the typical romantic location, but it is an alternative I urge you to seek out. After you've perused the aisles and selected a book together, you can sit around an open fireplace in one of the rooms and lose yourselves in your new literary find. The golden warmth from the fire helps set the mood for a spicy reading selection while you sip a cup of coffee and nibble one of the Thunderbird's fresh pastries. All this can add up to a perfect expenditure of time. (Dinner is served here also.)

ROBLES DEL RIO LODGE AND THE RIDGE RESTAURANT,
Carmel Valley   💋💋💋💋
200 Punta del Monte
(408) 659-3705
Inexpensive to Expensive

From Highway 1 take Carmel Valley Road to Esquiline and then follow the signs to the lodge.

Perched high in the hills above Carmel Valley, this rustic resort is everything you need for a genuine getaway from the rest of the world. You will feel somewhat isolated up here in the hills and forest, but the privacy is part of what makes this escape so exciting. *Robles del Rio* means "oaks of the river," and branches from these old trees cascade over terraced guest rooms that look out onto the California countryside. The rooms are more comfortable than they are elegant, ranging from one with a board-and-batten look to another with a Laura Ashley motif.

The dense woodland is fitting for a long, invigorating hike or lazy walk. When it finally comes time to lie around and do nothing, try their mountaintop Jacuzzi or heated pool. The pool is warm enough for swimming, and the breeze is cool enough to make you feel refreshed. If you dine at their **RIDGE RESTAURANT**, and you should, ask for a table on the glass-enclosed terrace. The food is excellent French cuisine and the view of the valley below is stunning.

STONEPINE, Carmel Valley
150 East Carmel Valley Road
(408) 659-2245
Very Expensive to Unbelievably Expensive

From Highway 1 take Carmel Valley Road east about 15 miles and watch for the sign on the right side of the road.

When the wrought-iron gate opened for us at Stonepine, we instantly had the feeling that something unforgettable was waiting for us within its grounds. Our anticipation intensified as we drove up the mile-long access road to the main house. Just past the entry we crossed a sturdy wooden bridge over a swiftly running creek. The entire way was lined with gnarled oak trees that sent streams of filtered sunlight through outstretched branches and fluttering leaves. Further ahead we noticed a couple touring the countryside in a horsedrawn carriage driven by a liveried coachman. In spite of our growing impatience to see what lay ahead at the chateau, we couldn't help but stop at the equestrian center we passed along the road. Vital, energetic horses galloped around the corral, which made it difficult to pull ourselves away. But no doubt there would be plenty of time to saddle up two horses of our own and explore some of Stonepine's prodigious 330 acres of forest, meadow and bridle trails.

When we finally reached the chateau, we embarked on a style of living that is hard to surpass. The spacious foyer and living room were filled with morning light that flowed in through a gallery of windows and enhanced the subtle elegance of the rose damask sofas and loveseats. A handwoven Chinese rug, threaded with the same rose tones, stretched across the hardwood floor, and golden flames gently caressed each other in an oversize stone hearth. Throughout the evening this room was graced by the sounds of a string ensemble.

There are 11 suites at Stonepine, each one with the same lavish appointments and exquisite detail as the public area. We were thoroughly delighted at everything we saw and experienced. Even the restaurant was a cornucopia of superb food and courtly service. Our first kiss at Stonepine was only the beginning of a truly magnificent weekend.

◆ **Romantic Alternative:** As long as we are on the subject of elite, posh places to stay (and there are several of those on the Monterey Peninsula), the **HIGHLAND INN**, Highway 1, (408) 624-3801 (Very Expensive to Unbelievably Expensive) is one more to consider. Less opulent then Stonepine, though still splendid, Highland Inn sits on an incredibly breathtaking expanse of coastline, and most of the contemporary-style rooms have fireplaces and lanais. The first-class restaurant has a first-class view and it is all very Californian and very wonderful and worth every moment you spend here.

BIG SUR

Located on Highway 1 about 150 miles south of San Francisco.

The drive from Carmel to Big Sur provides unsurpassed scenery in which to lose yourselves in an afternoon together. The road along this rugged, arduous coastline offers some of the most glorious, breathtaking views you may ever see in your life. It is almost guaranteed that once you've passed through Big Sur, its potent impact will be felt in your lives for years to come — it is that visually compelling. Take it slow through here — an experience of this magnitude needs to be approached with patient appreciation and reverent awe. Besides, there is no real destination to head for or to end up at, because there isn't an actual town of Big Sur to be found. According to the signs, though, Big Sur stretches for about six miles along Highway 1 and then continues south for more of the same impeccable scenery.

What makes all this such a heart throb? The road follows a precariously severe landscape, literally snaking its way along the unblemished shoreline. Beneath you, the relentless surf pounds the jagged outcroppings along the water's edge as nature continues to refine her sculpted masterpiece. Isolated beaches and secluded spots in the wilderness nearby provide momentary respite from the road for those who want to stop for private showcase views. Hard though it is to believe, each mile you pass through seems more remarkable and more titillating than the one before. Every moment you share here will be as seductive and as passionate as the first.

◆ *Romantic Suggestion:* Do not confuse **JULIA PFEIFFER BURNS STATE PARK** with Pfeiffer Big Sur State Park; Julia is only 11 miles further south than the other, but it offers what feels like 100 miles more privacy and landscape. Pfeiffer Big Sur State Park is exceedingly popular and disappointingly developed. Julia Burns State Park, on the other hand, is 2,000 acres of prime hiking territory in nature's virgin wonderland. Waterfalls, sequestered beaches and spellbinding views are what you can expect along the way. In the same vicinity, **PFEIFFER BEACH** (just off of Highway 1 on Sycamore Canyon Road) is an exhilarating seascape crowded with massive, eroded outcroppings and haystack rocks that are approachable during low tide. Watching the sunset from this vantage point is a life-altering proposition, it is that beautiful.

NEPENTHE, Big Sur
Highway 1
(408) 667-2345
Expensive

From San Francisco, take Highway 1 south till you reach Big Sur; there will be signs pointing you toward the restaurant.

Nepenthe is hardly a secret — you may even call it a tourist attraction of sorts. This famous restaurant, designed by a student of Frank Lloyd Wright, was the honeymoon cottage of Rita Hayworth and Orson Welles. It is also one of the few dining establishments to be found anywhere in Big Sur. What then makes it a kissing location? It is perched on a cliff 800 feet above the Big Sur shoreline. This feature alone is enough to make eating here a rapturous adventure.

Sunset is perhaps the best time to visit Nepenthe for a snack or drink. As the sun begins to settle into the ocean, its light penetrates the drifting clouds and casts over them a pale lavender-blue haze. Suddenly, these soft dusk-colors shift into an intense golden amber culminating in a deep red that sets the sky afire. As night makes its definitive entrance, the clouds fade to steel-blue and the sky turns from cobalt to indigo. Weather permitting, this floor show performs nightly along the Big Sur coast, and Nepenthe has some of the best seats in the house.

◆ *Romantic Suggestion:* The **GLEN OAKS RESTAURANT**, Highway 1, (408) 667-2623 (Moderate) doesn't have the view or the star-studded past of Nepenthe, but what it lacks in glamour it makes up for in charisma. Gourmet cuisine, a charming log cabin exterior and intimate candlelit interior are what makes Glen Oaks a ripe kissing location along Big Sur. (There's even morning kissing here: breakfast includes baked trout and fresh muffins.)

VENTANA, Big Sur
Highway 1
(408) 667-2331
Expensive to Unbelievably Expensive

Located on Highway 1 about 25 miles south of Carmel.

The unspoiled Santa Lucia Mountains seem to tumble directly into the sea. These rocky slopes and jagged outcroppings abut Big Sur's astonishing coastline. Ventana is an inn with a ringside view of all this, and its amenities will satisfy every other need you might have for a sultry weekend away from the world at large. Ventana is a retreat that is far removed from anything vaguely resembling civilization. Its rooms with raised ceilings, roaring fireplaces and sea-struck balconies are designed to direct your interests to romantic interactions. There are two heated pools, Japanese hot baths, a sauna and Jacuzzi. The guest rooms each have private patios or balconies that face the towering mountains or the endless ocean below. A short stroll from the inn, Ventana's restaurant offers another dramatic view of Big Sur. Outside, the fury of the ocean lashes the terrain under the terrace, while inside, yet another blazing fireplace provides solace and warmth. A stay here is a departure from the burdens and pressures of everyday living. The feelings that will fill your souls during your stay may surpass every expectation.

♦ *Romantic Note:* Bathing suits are considered optional attire around the pool.

> **"IT JUST TAKES AN ATTITUDE CHANGE TO TURN THE DELIRIUM INTO DELIGHT."**
>
> *Me*

THE CLAREMONT HOTEL AND TENNIS CLUB, Oakland
Ashby and Domingo Avenues
(415) 843-3000
Expensive to Unbelievably Expensive

From San Francisco, take the Bay Bridge to Highway 24 East. Exit at Claremont Avenue, turn left onto Claremont and then right on Ashby.

We almost always prefer a small, intimate hotel or bed & breakfast to a large flashy resort, even when the large flashy resort has everything we want. The problem with resorts is that they lend themselves to conventions and tour groups. There's something about feeling part of a software association's annual meeting that doesn't quite feel congenial or intimate. Besides, the facilities often tend to be crowded and the hot tub overflowing with people instead of water. As you may have already guessed, though, this famous hotel and tennis club is an exceptional exception to that rule.

Driving up Ashby Avenue, this majestic white stone mansion reminded us of villas we had seen in Europe. The exterior is epic in scale and style. The castle-like structure is surrounded by the Berkeley Hills and literally acres of deftly cultivated gardens and rows of endless palm trees. Outlining the horizon in the distance beyond the resort is one of the most impressive views of the San Francisco skyline to be seen anywhere.

Here at The Claremont, guests are encouraged to engage in any and all of the available outdoor activities. Tennis courts, an Olympic-size swimming pool and a nearby golf course offer an invigorating way to spend the day. Your personal energy level will be helped immensely by knowing that saunas and a hot tub are waiting for you inside. Following a full day of athletic playtime, you can indulge your whims again, only this time it can be at the **PAVILLION RESTAURANT**. This four-star dining room (we rated it a four-kiss experience) will seem even more satisfying after your long workout.

So where, you might wonder, is the romance in all of this athletic activity? We found it in the old-world architecture of the building, the cozy, yet grand accommodations that took us a lot further away from home than we expected. We felt it in the warmth of the sun as we tested our skill and took our time playing after a match or race. At The Claremont, romance is what you create from the physical workout of being together.

LAKE MERRITT, Oakland

From San Francisco, take the Bay Bridge to 880 south, then take the Broadway exit east until you reach Grand. Turn right. The street will eventually wind its way into the park.

Ask anyone in the East Bay area if downtown Oakland has any amorous potential and you'll probably hear the same answer: *"No!"* During my research, one person said, *"Oakland is a pit!"* This was brief but to the point. Then again, if you ask about Lake Merritt, people tend to whistle a different tune. Surrounded by Lakeside Park, Lake Merritt is located on 155 acres in, yes, downtown Oakland. Its surprising setting is an ideal place for picnicking, strolling, canoeing or any of a myriad of outdoor activities. Autumn is perhaps the best time to discover this city oasis. The leaves slowly change their colors and frame the lake in vibrant shades of gold and orange.

Start an afternoon here with a picnic near the water. Then try a sailing lesson or maybe take a tour on a minature sternwheeler. At **CHILDREN'S FAIRYLAND**, which attracts just as many adults as kids, puppet shows, a baby zoo, amusement rides and scenes from your favorite fairytales come alive and provide an ebullient diversion. Don't be too disappointed when you find the afternoon slipping away while so many sections of this domain remain unexplored. You'll have to return a few times to see it all, but that leaves you with something to look forward to next time you happen to be near downtown Oakland.

THE LOBBY, Oakland
5612 College Avenue
(415) 547-9152
Inexpensive

From San Francisco, take the Bay Bridge to Highway 24, then take the Claremont Avenue exit and cross over Claremont. Turn right onto Hudson and then left on College Avenue.

In my well-researched opinion, a piano bar can put you in the mood for something more than just listening to music. Not that tableside swaying to the rhythms isn't rousing all by itself, but somehow, when all the right details are right, a visit to a piano bar can be one of the best romantic escapades you'll ever have. That is what you'll likely find happens at The Lobby. This hideaway is filled with lots of Tiffany lamps, Victorian loveseats and, of course, the grand piano. Dulcet tunes and more boisterous sing-alongs offer a little something for every musical taste. It's the kind of place that puts the finishing touches on a night out on the town.

BERKELEY ROSE GARDEN

From San Francisco, take the Bay Bridge and stay on Highway 80 going north. Take the University exit and turn right. Go straight to Shattuck Avenue and turn left. At Hearst Street turn right. From here your last turn is a left on Euclid, which you follow to the top of the hill.

The Berkeley Rose Garden is an enchanting realm filled with evolving color and fragrance. From its upper level, you gaze over an amphitheatre of nature's glory. Then as you make your way down the stairs, passing one rosebush after another, the sweet air and the flawless surrounding beauty will encompass you. This is prime kissing territory, acre after beautiful acre. The sedate setting is so expansive that even when others are around, you can almost always find an empty bench waiting for just the two of you. Here you can sit very close together and spend a few moments (or hours) in a location that feels like paradise.

CHEZ PANISSE, Berkeley
1517 Shattuck Avenue
(415) 548-5525
Expensive

French restaurants are not automatically categorized as romantic by the standards used for The Best Places To Kiss rating system. Granted, the lighting and mood are often right, but more is needed than linen tablecloths, a French accent and a Julia Child wannabe in the kitchen. We are very careful not to let white linen and pastel Waterford china be our only criteria. Having explained all that, suffice it to say that Chez Panisse is as stellar a dining experience as any two hearts and two gourmet appetites could want.

Many restaurant reviewers say that if you eat out only once in San Francisco, Chez Panisse should be the place — and it just happens to be in Berkeley. Well, far be it from me to argue with the edible truth. If unsurpassed French gourmet is your idea of a fabulous romantic meal and you happpen to be on the other side of the bridge (and you can get reservations), the food and atmosphere will indeed be the best ever.

◆ *Romantic Warning:* Did I mention that you may have to book your reservations weeks, if not months, in advance, particularly if you want to dine on a weekend? Also, the staff tends to be a bit on the stuffy side — well they wouldn't call it stuffy, they'd call it professional. I suppose it depends on your point of view.

◆ *Romantic Option:* If you find there is no way you can get into Chez Panisse, you will not be disappointed if you try **RESTAURANT METROPOLE**, 2271 Shattuck Avenue, (415) 848-3080 (Moderate). The Metropole has a truly warm French country inn ambience and the food is beautifully prepared. Fresh flowers grace the room and a pianist plays classical music. This place is hard to pass up, even if you do get reservations for the abovementioned culinary extravaganza.

GRAMMA'S INN, Berkeley
2740 Telegraph Avenue
(415) 549-2145
Moderate to Expensive

From San Francisco, take the Bay Bridge east and then stay on Highway 80 to the Ashby Avenue exit. Turn right on Ashby and then make a left on Telegraph Avenue.

Sometimes you simply want a place to stay that's comfortable and cozy. A place designed for cuddling, without pretense or affectation. Gramma's Inn is one of those kind of places. It's not what I would call a notably amorous-sounding name, but then what's in a name besides letters?

This Tudor-style bed & breakfast is actually two skillfully restored mansions in a neighborhood that should take the hint and do renovations of its own. All of the rooms have been lovingly enhanced with antique furnishings and thick handsewn quilts. Some of the suites overlook the garden, others have private decks or fireplaces, and another includes stained glass windows that encompass the entire room. There is also the likelihood that "Gramma" will spoil you beyond repair. Milk and cookies are set out in the afternoon and a respectable breakfast of baked breads and homemade preserves are served in the morning. The only romantic warning here is that some of the rooms share baths. Be sure to ask for one with private facilities if that's part of your kissing requirement.

◆ *Romantic Option:*Gramma's Inn is so close to the University of California at Berkeley that you shouldn't miss the opportunity to see this beautiful campus. It is a lovely place for a picnic, particularly in the summer when the student population dwindles significantly.

THE SHATTUCK HOTEL, Berkeley
2086 Allston Way
(415) 845-7300
Inexpensive to Moderate

From San Francisco take the Bay Bridge and stay on Highway 80 to University Avenue and turn right. When you reach Shattuck Avenue turn right again. The hotel is on the corner of Shattuck and Allston Way.

If you are spending time in Berkeley and require a peaceful place away from the hustle and bustle of this town's quaint but busy streets, The Shattuck Hotel would be a premier choice. It is located in the midst of all the activity, but once inside you'll feel as if you've entered a refuge where matters of the heart are tended to with style and care. The attractive lobby is decorated with Victorian furnishings, dark wood paneling, white columns and subtle lighting. The guest rooms are comfortable and stately. This historical landmark has been renovated with just the right balance of modern amenities to make it a tasteful blend of two opposing worlds.

◆ *Romantic Note:* Plan to have at least one meal at **SEDONA'S**, (415) 841-3848. This Southwestern-style restaurant is connected to the hotel. The food is outstanding and it is served in a dining room with an architectural flare and decor that is difficult to equal.

SKATES ON THE BAY, Berkeley
100 Seawall Drive at the University
(415) 549-1900
Moderate

From San Francisco take the Bay Bridge and stay on I80 north to the University exit. Make a (legal) U-turn at the first stoplight and head back in the opposite direction. You will come to a fork in the road at the marina. Stay to your left and where the road dead-ends, turn right into the restaurant's parking lot.

San Francisco has one of the world's most stunning skylines. One of the ways to really appreciate it is to go to Berkeley and look back across the water where you can take in the entire view. From here you can observe the Golden City's sensational personality, marked by the expansive blue bay and steep urban hills lined with steel-and-glass skyscrapers. Skates on the Bay has just such a panoramic view and it is without question dazzling. Thank goodness the food is good and the interior is a respectable blend of modern and quaint. You'll be tempted to stay for dessert so you can linger over the city's lights and each other's company a little longer.

LAFAYETTE PARK HOTEL, Lafayette
3287 Mount Diablo Boulevard
(415) 283-3700
Moderate to Expensive

From San Francisco take the Bay Bridge to Highway 24, then take the Pleasant Hill Road exit to Mount Diablo Boulevard and turn right.

From the freeway it looked like a French chalet, which was impressive, but it was visible from the highway and that worried me. After all, a love nest that borders highways or busy roads is potentially a pigeonhole when it comes to romance. In this case, however, my skepticism was unfounded. The moment our weekend at Lafayette

Park Hotel began, I forgot the freeway even existed.

High above the lobby, skylights illuminate a handcarved staircase that winds its way down three stories. A profusion of fresh flowers brought soft color and life to the elegant decor. This same feeling existed throughout the hotel, including our brightly appointed room. Ours had a vaulted ceiling and a woodburning fireplace. We were thoroughly pleased. Exploring further, we found three charming courtyards. One was built around an Italian marble fountain, another surrounded a stone wishing-well, the third had a large swimming pool and whirlpool spa. Adjacent to the lobby is the **DUCK CLUB RESTAURANT**, offering an admirable dining experience. After dinner, a latte or capuccino in the lounge, near the cobblestone fireplace, was a wonderful way to round out the evening.

TOURELLE'S, Lafayette
3565 Mount Diablo Boulevard
(415) 284-3565
Moderate

From San Francisco take the Bay Bridge to Highway 24. Take the Central Lafayette exit and make a right at the end of the off-ramp, then another right onto Mount Diablo Boulevard.

A stone path takes you past the garden to an ivy-covered tower and two brick homes that surround a charming courtyard with a pond at its center. Here is an engaging place for lunch on a warm, leisurely afternoon. On one side of the courtyard is an informal bistro with a big, open kitchen. On the other is a beautiful dining room with towering vaulted ceilings, brick walls and delectable French food. Dining at Tourelle's can make you feel as if you are in the south of France, which is a fairly terrific feeling to share with someone special.

LE VIRAGE, Walnut Creek
2211 North Main Street
(415) 933-8484
Expensive

From San Fancisco take the Bay Bridge to Highway 24 and then to 680 north. Take the North Main Street exit and turn left. The restaurant is a few blocks ahead on your left.

Driving down the streets of Walnut Creek, you may be surprised to find a charming little farmhouse at *le virage* (*"a bend in the road"*). Surrounded by glass and cement, this city oasis is a startling contrast to its many officious neighbors. Le Virage is a restaurant that serves excellent continental cuisine in a setting that whisks you away from modern-day business life, and the hectic pace that accompanies it will disappear once you enter. The mood is one of nostalgic, unhurried romance.

♦ *Romantic Option:* MAXIMILLIAN'S, 1604 Locust Street, (415) 932-1474 (Moderate to Expensive). There are two dining rooms at Maximillian's, each sporting its own menu and decor. Upstairs, oak paneling and bricks blend to create a handsome, formal atmosphere for classic continental dinners. The downstairs is done in softer shades of dusty rose and mint green, where a contemporary menu of California nouvelle cuisine is served. Both are congenial spots for an evening interlude.

> **"TO BE IN LOVE IS TO BE IN
> A STATE OF PERPETUAL ANAESTHESIA."**
> *H.L. Mencken*

CASA MADRONA HOTEL & RESTAURANT, Sausalito
801 Bridgeway
Hotel (415) 332-0502
Moderate to Very Expensive

Heading over to Marin County on Highway 101, take the first exit (Alexander Avenue) after you cross the Golden Gate Bridge. This winding road proceeds downhill and then automatically connects to Bridgeway. The hotel is located on the left side of the road, after the second traffic light in the town.

Casa Madrona is one meandering surprise after another. The rooms display the creative work of no fewer than 16 local designers, and each one is more interesting than the next. As you climb to your room on the tiered walkway, this multi-layered hotel will reveal every sort of style from blushingly romantic to endearingly strange. A description of each of the rooms at Casa Madrona would require a book by itself. You name it and you can find it here, in a variety of compositions and arrangements: spacious to cozy, French country to contemporary modern, brilliant sunlit harbor views to skylights to fireplaces and on and on. The two of you only need to decide what your composite is going to be.

If an overnight stay is not possible, the restaurant at Casa Madrona is a heart-stirring alternative. The dining area has a remarkable panoramic view of Sausalito Bay; all the refreshments outside the windows will beautifully complement your meal inside. After you've dined, take a stroll hand-in-hand through the town of Sausalito. Or, if you have decided to stay at the hotel, you can stroll back to your private, individualized haven at Casa Madrona.

◆ *Romantic Suggestion:* One of the ways to get to Sausalito or Tiburon and not get stuck in street traffic is to take the ferry. The **GOLDEN GATE FERRY**, (415) 332-6600 leaves from the San

Francisco Ferry Building, located at the foot of Market Street, and makes its way across the bay every day of the week. The more romantic times are off-peak hours during most weekdays, but even when the boat is thick with commuters, this is a genuinely San Franciscan way to sightsee in the Bay Area.

ALTA MIRA RESTAURANT, Sausalito
125 Buckley Avenue
(415) 332-1350
Expensive to Very Expensive

Heading over to Marin County on Highway 101, take the first exit (Alexander Avenue) after you cross the Golden Gate Bridge. This winding road proceeds downhill and then automatically connects to Bridgeway. Once you enter the town of Sausalito, turn right on Bay Street to Buckley Avenue. Turn right and follow the signs to Alta Mira.

A more impressive location for brunch or an afternoon nosh would be hard to find. Tucked away on a hillside overlooking Richardson Harbor and the San Francisco skyline, this terraced restaurant is the prime spot for a leisurely meal together. The view from up here is so vibrant that it becomes an integral part of the interior. Leave yourselves plenty of time to take in the entire landscape.

♦ *Romantic Warning:* The Alta Mira is also well-known for its hotel accommodations, though why anyone would want to stay here is beyond me. The hotel has been in desperate need of renovations since the 1960s; the rooms are tacky, the floors creak, the bathrooms aren't big enough for one person, let alone two, and there is a mildewy smell throughout that is fairly unpleasant. Our suggestion is to stay elsewhere and enjoy the view from the restaurant during breakfast, lunch or dinner.

SCOMA'S, Sausalito
558 Bridgeway
(415) 332-9551
Moderate

See the directions for Casa Madrona into Sausalito. Once you enter the town, continue on Bridgeway to the restaurant on the right side of the road.

Classic seafood dishes are served in a very pretty, very classic dining environment that is made even more enticing by its dynamite location on the shore of Sausalito. The view from the glass-enclosed room is breathtaking regardless of the weather. After dinner, a walk along the shore to watch the moon's reflection on the water is a spectacular way to end your evening.

◆ *Romantic Alternative:* HORIZON'S, 558 Bridgeway, (415) 331-3232 (Moderate) has a casual atmosphere that offers the same outstanding, expansive view as Scoma's. The dark-wooded interior is fronted by a wall of windows that open onto a deck poised directly over the bay. From here you can survey the entire area from the Bay Bridge to the home-covered hills of Tiburon. A hot cup of coffee or cocktail from this vantage point can turn out to be an inspiring affair.

CAPRICE RESTAURANT, Tiburon
2000 Paradise Drive
(415) 435-3400
Moderate to Expensive

Once you enter the town of Tiburon, follow Paradise Drive along the water for about 3 miles. The restaurant will be on your right.

This restaurant would delight the most finicky of gourmands. The Caprice is a divinely quaint place with a reclusive hobbit-like aura. The homey wood-framed structure sits snug on a stone embankment above the gently swirling waters of Raccoon Strait looking across to Angel Island. The small dining salon is warmed by a radiating fireplace, and the large windows allow perfect ringside water viewing. It would be difficult for you not to give in to the loving atmosphere this place generates.

♦ *Romantic Suggestion:* After brunch or an early dinner at The Caprice, continue up Paradise Drive till you reach **PARADISE BEACH PARK**. This quiet little corner of the world is a wooded landscape that overlooks the distant hills beyond the bay and the San Rafael Bridge. Depending on the time of day and season, this place could be yours alone, and there is enough strolling and picnicking turf here to make it a lover's point of interest.

♦ *Second Romantic Suggestion:* **SAN RAFAEL AVENUE** in Tiburon wraps around a cove that has a simply glorious view of the sunset. You can walk slowly along this neighborhood street and watch the fading colors of day as they surrender to nightfall.

LARK CREEK INN, Larkspur
234 Magnolia Avenue
(415) 924-7766
Moderate

Take Highway 101 to the Paradise Drive/Mount Tamalpais Exit. Go west on Mount Tamalpais for about 1 mile, turning right on Corte Madera Avenue which becomes Magnolia Avenue. The restaurant is a half mile down on the right.

As you wind through the remote wooded neighborhoods of Larkspur, you will be surprised to see this yellow frame home on what would otherwise be another curve in an out-of-the-way country road. Though this place feels remote, it is one of the more renowned dining spots in the North Bay. Lark Creek Inn deserves its reputation and, in spite of its popularity, the environment is still conducive to a romantic interlude. The interior is highlighted by a glass-domed ceiling shaded by lofty redwoods. When the weather warms, the restaurant's garden, situated near a babbling creek, serves as an extension to the dining room. The only thing left to mention is the food, which is sheer heaven most of the time; when its not, then its merely excellent.

RODEO BEACH AT THE MARIN HEADLANDS ❤❤❤
(415) 331-1540

Head north from San Francisco on Highway 101. Take the Alexander Avenue exit and follow the signs to Golden Gate National Recreation Area. At Bunker Road contine 3 miles to the beach.

This expanse of white sandy beach is not a secret to locals, but you can be effectively alone during most weekdays before summer vacation releases eager kids from the classroom. A more beautiful scenic area for rambling through surf cannot be found so near to San Francisco. Colored stones of jasper and agate are scattered along the shore. Bird Island, just a short distance from shore, is often blanketed with fluttering white birds. In the distance, rolling hills and jagged cliffs make distinguished tableaux against the bright blue sky. There are plenty of hiking trails nearby that lead you over intriguing terrain to breathtaking overviews of the area. You will not be at a loss for ways to spend time here; you only need to be prepared for sun, wind and long, loving hours together.

♦ *Romantic Note:* **GOLDEN GATE NATIONAL RECREA-TION AREA**, (415) 331-1540 contains over 70,000 acres of protected coastline, pristine woodland, mountain terrain, rugged hillsides and meticulously maintained city parks. To say that there is a diverse assortment of places to discover here is at best an understatement. It seems hard to believe that such a massive refuge can exist so close to San Francisco. Hiking, picnicking, swimming or any other outdoor activity you can think of is available in this awesome stretch of land. There is something here for the most ardent wilderness lovers and the most tame urban dwellers. It is simply there for your pleasure, provided by Mother Nature and the Golden Gate National Park Association.

MUIR WOODS AND MOUNT TAMALPAIS
Panoramic Highway
(415) 388-2070

Take the Golden Gate Bridge (which is Highway 101) to Marin County.
From Highway 101 take the Stinson Beach/Highway 1 exit, following the
signs for Muir Woods and Mount Tamalpais.

If you're longing to be secluded and near nature, you only need to
cross the Golden Gate Bridge into Marin County and drive along
Highway 1 to the crest of Mount Tamalpais. This is without question
one of the most absorbing drives the area has to bestow. The S-curved
road coils along the edge of this windswept highland and each turn
exposes another vantage point from which to scan the scenery —
land cascading down to Marin, and the pattern of overlapping hills.
As you continue your excursion, you can choose to remain in the
car or venture out into the hills with a *fête champêtre* (picnic) in
hand. Here in the midst of earth's simple gifts, a loaf of bread, a jug
of wine and thou are all you need.

♦ *Romantic Suggestion:* The **STEEP RAVINE TRAIL**, whose
trailhead is at the Pantoll Station on the Panoramic Highway, is a
magnificent deep-forest journey to views of the ocean and bay. This
one is my sister's romantic favorite, and she ought to know: the idea
for this book was hers.

♦ *Romantic Suggestion:* **MOUNTAIN HOME INN**, 810
Panoramic Highway, Mill Valley, (415) 381-9000 (Moderate to
Expensive) is situated on the north side of Mount Tamalpais, standing
guard over the surrounding East Bay hills, the Tiburon peninsula,
San Francisco and Mount Diablo. It is a handsome, refurbished lodge
where the excellent food and sublime views combine to create a rare
treat among dining experiences. There are also 10 cozy guest rooms
at the inn, several of which boast their own fireplace, Jacuzzi and
deck. Regardless of which room is yours, all have views of purple
mountain majesty.

THE PELICAN INN RESTAURANT AND PUB, Muir Beach
(415) 383-6000
Moderate

Twenty minutes from the Golden Gate Bridge on Highway 1. Take Highway 101 over the bridge into Marin County. Exit at Stinson Beach/Highway 1. Follow the signs for Muir Woods, which lead you directly to the inn.

Among the redwoods, between the pines and alders, dabbed with touches of honeysuckle and jasmine, is The Pelican Inn, a magical place out of the past. This 16th-century-style country cottage, hidden in the Golden Gate National Recreational Area, is a shelter for the weary, hungry traveler, as well as the habitat for the "little folk" of days gone by. All this will be clearly evident as you approach the inn, especially when the weather assists in the magic. Sea mist often mingles with the mountain air to create a foggy veil that contributes to the sense that you are moving back through time to England of Olde.

You can take your schooner of ale or pot of tea to a table near the stone hearth of the brick fireplace and allow this daydream to continue for as long as you dare. Or you can simply snuggle close together, watching the embers flicker and glow in the dimly lit room as you wait for the innkeeper to bring you your afternoon or evening feast.

♦ *Romantic Warning:* The guest rooms in The Pelican Inn are called "rustic" by the owners, but from our point of view "run down" would be a more descriptive word. If you happen to be in a pioneer frame of mind, the rooms could pass muster. Besides, there are the mystical, cinematic setting and acres of forest and nearby beaches to stimulate your imagination.

♦ *Romantic Possibility:* Nearby **MUIR BEACH STATE PARK** is a well-frequented expanse of white sandy shoreline, which means that too much smooching is probably out of the question. That doesn't mean you can't claim your own spot, lay back, listen to the ocean's serene rhythms and concentrate on each other.

POINT REYES NATIONAL SEASHORE
(415) 663-1092

I'm usually of the opinion that statistics are not in the least bit romantic. They're great if you feel like absorbing data, but they won't create a groundwork for snuggling. For example, if you know that Point Reyes National Seashore has geologically noteworthy formations and protected wildlife, it may not do much for you. What may entice you more is knowing that you are likely to fall in love with acre after exquisite acre of wildland, colored by winter grass, patterned with chiseled rock, cascading waterfalls, calm sandy beaches, precarious primitive coastline and turbulent eddies of water crashing against haystock rocks spewing streams of water into the fresh air above. Now that has meaning! You can almost feel the ground move under your quickening feet as you see ahead the crest of a ridge while you traverse one of the many trails that interlace this prime hiking kingdom. At the end of some trails, you'll find yourselves standing near the edge of land, where the ocean reveals itself nestled between interwoven hills. Regain your composure. Now is the moment to create lasting memories.

The number of spectacular treks in this area is too great to list in this book. Realistically, not everyone who wants to find romance owns hiking boots, or for that matter, thighs and a disposition that can handle the job. For a beautifully written examination of the hikes available, I strongly recommend the book **Point Reyes Secret Places and Magic Moments**, by Phil Arnot. His descriptions and instructions are accurate and fairly easy to follow.

◆ *Romantic Suggestion:* Three of my favorite places in Point Reyes National Seashore are **ALAMERE FALLS, TOMALES POINT,** and **WILDCAT BEACH.** Each is dramatically different from the other, and the natural glory that exists here is worth discovering for yourselves. Check with the ranger station for hiking information about these areas, or use the book by Phil Arnot I mentioned above.

♦ *Second Romantic Suggestion:* **FIVE BROOKS STABLES,**
(415) 663-8287 is a fabulous horse ranch with hourly rentals at Point
Reyes National Seashore.

♦ *Romantic Warning:* The town of Inverness, which borders the
Point Reyes National Seashore, is the entry point into this area. Even
though this wee-small village is somewhat quaint, it is too well-
traveled to be a truly romantic option all by itself. However, a stay
at one of the special bed & breakfasts mentioned in the next few
entries can be utterly romantic. For more information regarding
accommodations, both romantic and not so romantic, you can write
to **Inns of Point Reyes**, P.O. Box 145, Inverness, CA 94937 for a
copy of their brochure.

WHALE WATCHING

From numerous viewpoints along the Coast Trail in the Point Reyes
National Seashore, and especially from Point Reyes Lighthouse (415)
669-1534 at the end of Sir Francis Drake Boulevard due west of Inverness.

If you have always secretly longed to witness firsthand the passage
of whales on their yearly migration to warmer waters, then the
Northern California Coast is a great place to live out your underwater
fantasy. December to April is the best time to witness this odyssey,
particularly when the weather conditions are clear and sunny. Be
sure to go early in the morning, about the time when the sun is
radiantly warming the cool morning air. As you stand at the edge of
a cliff towering over the depths below, you will have a tremendous
view of this tortuous coastline. Find a comfortable position, snuggle
close together, and be patient. This performance is intermittent at
best and requires careful study and diligence. Be prepared for an
amazing encounter.

Imagine, for as far as the eye can see, the open, endless ocean
lined with staggered cliffs, haloed with green and gold chaparral.
Allow your vision to slowly scan the calm, flowing blue waters. Then

suddenly, in the distance, breaking the still of a silent, sun-drenched spring morning, a spout of bursting water explodes from the surface. A giant, arched black profile appears boldly against the blue sea, followed by an abrupt tail slap and then stillness once more. It's hard to explain the romance of that moment, but romantic it is. Perhaps it's the excitement of observing such an immense creature gliding effortlessly through the water with playful agility and ease. Or perhaps it's the chance you have to celebrate a part of nature's mysterious aquatic underworld together.

MACLEAN HOUSE, Inverness
P.O. Box 651
(415) 669-7392
Inexpensive

From the town of Inverness, on Highway 1, turn left on Inverness Highway. Go 2 short blocks and take a sharp right on Hawthornden Way. MacLean House is on your left as you go up the hill, but Hawthornden is a divided road, so you must make a U-turn at the top and come back down to the parking area.

This charming bed & breakfast is 2 blocks from the main street of Inverness and only minutes from the ocean. As you drive up the road you will see the house set upon a hill. It is a brick-and-stone dwelling, set amidst gardens and trees. There are only 2 guest rooms in this Scottish-style guesthouse, and both are homespun and uncomplicated. Before or after a hard day of combing the seashore hand-in-hand, you can lounge on the trellised deck where breakfast and afternoon tea are served along with shortbreads and sherry. As you recline on the terrace, you'll see in the distance Tomales Bay framing the horizon in picturesque harmony with the landscape.

◆ *Romantic Suggestion:* Along the western edge of Tomales Bay, in Tomales Bay State Park, is **HEART'S DESIRE BEACH**. It's worth a visit. Even if you believe that names have no meaning, it still may be interesting to test the truth of this one for yourselves.

♦ *Romantic Alternative:* **THE NEON ROSE**, (415) 663-9143 (Expensive) is an amazingly unique cottage on a hill overlooking Tomales Bay. You walk through a delightful, small, very private garden and into your own modern white stucco-and-wood little cottage. The view from up here is a broad vista of Point Reyes and the bay. It has a fully equipped kitchen, a chic bedroom opening onto a cozy living area with a Jacuzzi tub, woodstove and complete stereo system. If only home were like this! The Neon Rose bed & breakfast is the ultimate in privacy. You could stay here for days and feel blissfully content.

♦ *Second Romantic Alternative:* **DANCING COYOTE BEACH GUEST COTTAGES**, 12794 Sir Francis Drake Boulevard, (415) 669-7200 (Moderate) are nestled in the shade of sturdy pine and cypress trees on Tomales Bay. Each cottage has access to private beachfront a few feet from its front door. Fireplaces, skylights, floor-to-ceiling windows and pastel colors of green and peach adorn each bungalow. This getaway is made to order when you're in need of time to jointly embrace tranquility.

HIGHWAY 1

The Northern California Coast Highway 1, mile after mile, is an exhilarating roller coaster ride of a lifetime. The road writhes its way along terrain that would otherwise seem impassable. Following the ocean from atop towering cliffs, each turn capriciously switches back on itself, following the edge so closely that you may feel more like you're hang-gliding than motoring along. At other times, you'll feel the ocean mist on your face and hear the roar of the surf and you may think you're boating instead of just driving.

Be sure to allow enough time to travel this highway at a leisurely, touring pace. There are scads of turnoffs that will demand your attention, so the slower your speed, the easier it will be to stop at any given point and enjoy. The picture-perfect profile of the pounding surf against death-defying palisades continues on forever. Each corner, each turn, has a view so like Eden that a kissing warning seems in order: *Driving and kissing don't mix!* Before you indulge, be sure you are parked and not negotiating the narrow turns on Highway 1.

◆ **Romantic Warning:** If you are in a hurry to get to points north at a faster clip, do yourselves and the rest of the traffic on Highway 1 a favor and take Highway 101.

THE INN AT VALLEY FORD, Valley Ford
14395 Highway 1
(707) 876-3182
Moderate

On Highway 1, just south of Bodega Bay, on the west side of the road.

Bed & breakfasts each have a characteristic brand of cordial, cozy warmth; that is the earmark of this genre of lodging. Given the right touches, there is nothing quite as affection-producing as staying someplace that diligently attends to matters of the heart. This means the aroma of fresh-baked scones and croissants, a well-tended fireplace, cushy antique decor, snuggly quilts piled with oversized pillows, sizable rooms, and a conspicuous amount of responsive loving care. The Inn at Valley Ford has seen to all that and more. The one drawback to this place is its communal bathroom facilities. There is something disconcerting about running into someone you don't know en route to the powder room, or worse, finding it occupied when you're in need. The reason we make an exception to our policy in this case is because one of the shared bathrooms here is a suite unto itself. In fact, you may decide to stay in there and forget about returning to your own room. The feature that will surely spark your interest is the large, tiled, walk-down shower which is large enough to qualify as a small playfield. With space to spare, it can accommodate two people who want to emerge clean, giggling and inseparable.

RIVER'S END RESTAURANT, Jenner

Highway 1
(707) 865-2484
Moderate to Expensive

On the west side of Highway 1, just north of the town of Jenner.

The view of swirling whitewater and turbulent eddies that explode over and around the rock outcroppings of the Pacific Ocean can change at night into a placid almost surreal composition. As sunset nears, a single path of sunlight glosses the surface, illuminating only the water and the horizon, with the hills veiled in darkness. Evening announces its finale with a crescendo of colors that fade slowly to black. From the deck and dining room of River's End Restaurant, this daily, sparkling performance is open to behold. If you've timed it right, nightfall and the last taste of your succulent, well-prepared dinner will occur simultaneously. Whether taking care of your appetite or spending a starry-eyed evening together is what you had in mind, both desires will be fully sated.

♦ *Romantic Note:* The days and hours that the restaurant are open vary depending on the season.

♦ *Romantic Warning:* River's End is also a lodge with guest rooms that have the same view as the restaurant, only closer to the water. Why the warning? Because the decor can only be described as tacky and old, which makes the rooms hardly romantic. The price and scenery are certainly desirable, so if proximity to the ocean and bargain accommodations are paramount concerns, this place is a gem.

♦ *Romantic Alternative:* **JENNER BY THE SEA**, Coast Highway 1 at Jenner, (707) 865-1192 (Moderate) in any other setting might be considered a little too rustic or too casual and too near the highway for a romantic dinner. Here on the Sonoma Coast, however, almost any restaurant with a large fireplace and hearth, windows that survey the meandering Russian River emptying into the Pacific, and a kitchen staff that prepares very fresh seafood dishes is indeed a special spot.

FORT ROSS LODGE, Jenner
20705 Highway 1
(707) 847-3333
Inexpensive to Expensive

On the west side of Highway 1, just north of Jenner.

The setting for this place is impeccable. The main building rests on a rocky pinnacle that pirouettes above the rugged azure sea and is encircled by rolling meadows dotted with wildflowers and dried golden brush. Nearby are dense woodlands of redwood and fir trees that house a newer, upscale section of the lodge. Each of the rooms bordering the ocean has sliding glass doors that open onto a private deck overlooking the unobstructed beauty of the Pacific. A glass-enclosed hot tub with the same view is available for guests, and many rooms come with their own sizable soaking tub for more private, interpersonal use. Even the price is more than reasonable for such a stellar location: In spite of all this, I'm not certain Fort Ross Lodge is really romantic; the rooms are quite tacky — lumpy, sagging beds, ugly brown carpeting, secondhand furnishings and a VCR in each room (for kissing purposes a VCR is not considered to be a heart-tugging feature). But then again, there's that view and your own private deck. I guess you'll have to decide for yourselves, because I can't seem to make up my mind.

TIMBERHILL COUNTRY INN & TENNIS RANCH, Cazadero
35755 Hauser Bridge Road
(707) 847-3258
Unbelievably Expensive

Five miles north of Jenner, turn right onto Meyers Grade Road (first right after Seaview Plantation Road) and make your climb to the ridge. This is a country road that you follow for 13.7 miles from Highway 1. Six miles down, the Meyers Grade Road turns into Seaview and then Seaview turns into Hauser Bridge Road, which ends at the ranch.

Why would a tennis ranch be considered a perfect place to unite in a soul-connecting embrace? After all, if you don't like cuddling a racquet and have anxiety about chasing balls in the hot afternoon sun, you're probably thinking of ignoring this selection altogether. But be open-minded. At this ranch, if you can't tell a tennis racquet from a baseball bat you can still enjoy it, because all around you will be 80 wooded acres of nature's finest greenery far removed from the pressures of the real world. The ranch is home to 10 handsome cedar-log cabins all with the appropriate romantic requirements: fireplace, views, sundeck and extreme privacy. From your own patio you can watch the sunset paint the country hills with a kaleidoscope of color. Even the dining room has its own serene elegance that adds to the enticing meals, all presented by a time-honored chef. The acres of woodland that ramble on endlessly next to the ranch will tempt you to take long hikes. Or stay on the grounds and swim, or relax in the Jacuzzi till the day journeys into night and dinnertime nears. If you want to get far enough away from civilization to create some country magic, then Timberhill Ranch may be your answer.

◆ *Romantic Note:* The daily room rate here includes all meals.

EMPIRE CAFE, Gualala
Gualala, CA 95445
(707) 884-4630
Inexpensive to Moderate

As you come into Gualala on Highway 1, the restaurant is on the west side of the road.

In real estate the most important thing is location, location, location. That statement holds true for the Empire Cafe. Perched on one of the most spectacular bluffs overlooking the Sonoma Coast, this restaurant's view would merit an exceptional romantic rating even if it just served coffee. From the outside there is absolutely no indication of what lies inside. The parking lot is dusty and the facade is grey knotty wood — nice but unimpressive. The only clue to what lies within is when you glance around the building's exterior and see the continuous view of the ocean and sky colors merging in peaceful unison. Once you venture inside, the mood is bright and very Californian. The back of the cafe is wall-to-wall windows with a wraparound deck. Optimum seating on a warm, clear day is out here where you can feel the breeze lift the sea air all around you.

♦ *Romantic Note:* Be sure to dress warmly, because even when the sun is directly overhead a cool breeze here can feel like a cold shower.

ST. ORRES INN AND RESTAURANT, Gualala
P.O. Box 523
(707) 884-3303
Inexpensive to Expensive

As you head north out of Gualala on Highway 1, the spires of St. Orres will appear on the left. If you reach Anchor Bay, you have gone too far.

Finding words that succinctly express the richness and architectural intrigue of this bed & breakfast is a challenge. Your hearts and thoughts will succumb to the dream world you enter here at St. Orres. Rising above a cloistered sandy cove, this structure appears suddenly out of nowhere, a fascinating handcarved wood-and-glass Russian-style chalet. The stained glass windows of the inn's two intricately crafted towers twinkle at you in the daylight. This same prismatic light bathes the interior of the inn in a velvety amber hue. On the main floor, the distinctive dining room uses the light to its full potential: It adorns a petite indoor arboretum. The food is also a culinary treat. The guest rooms here are varied, from simple to splendid; there are even cottages scattered about the grounds, each with its own spirit and tone. Some have a perfect unobstructed ocean view, others have sundecks, fireplaces and sunken tubs. Whatever you finally settle on at St. Orres, your own dream world is guaranteed to come quickly alive.

◆ *Romantic Suggestion:* There are several beaches accessible from Highway 1. Keep watch for the signs, as they pop up inconsistently. **SHELL BEACH**, just south of Gualala, is one of those windswept beaches you reach via a tree-covered trail. Beachcombing along here is a wonderful way to spend an afternoon.

THE OLD MILANO HOTEL, Gualala
38300 Highway 1
(707) 884-3256
Moderate to Expensive

The hotel is 1 mile north of the town of Gualala, on Highway 1. Watch for a small, easily missed sign for the hotel on the west side of the road.

This modest turn-of-the-century bed & breakfast has an irresistible quality. It is unsurpassed for its invitation to modern gracious living and its enthusiasm for country finery. Every corner — the dining area, suites, furnishings, and gardens — all reflect a heartfelt tenderness. As you turn from the road down the sandy driveway to the main house, you will readily appreciate the enveloping seclusion.

The main building and the adjoining cottages are settled on a 3-acre estate with the ocean only a stone's throw from the front door. At night, safe in the confines of your own shelter, the sound of the surf will lull you to sleep. In the morning, after a late, lazy breakfast of freshly baked breads and an assortment of other delicacies, you can stroll along the shore and look back at the slice of heaven the two of you found together.

◆ *Romantic Note:* Be sure to ask about the caboose accommodations if you want a totally different, romantically bawdy adventure.

WHALE WATCH INN, Gualala
35100 Highway 1
(707) 884-3667
Expensive to Very Expensive

On Highway 1 just north of Gualala, on the west side of the road.

Most modern hotels or resorts remind me of suburban condominium developments — functional, but not very romantic. On the other hand, there is something about newness that can sometimes be inventive, fresh, and artistic. When you take innovative architecture and combine it with a thrilling setting, you will be standing in front of Whale Watch Inn. The inn oversees the rugged, treacherous shoreline and sandy beach inlet of Anchor Bay. The music of the rushing water resounds through the 5 compact buildings that comprise this complex. The wood exterior is stained a weathered seaside gray that harmonizes with the landscape. The inn boasts only 18 suites, each with its own flair. Skylights, sundecks, whirlpools and fireplaces are enhanced by plush furnishings and pastel fabrics. There is an overpowering air of loving feeling here that will influence your stay and inevitably encourage you to return.

◆ *Romantic Footnote:* Each room at Whale Watch contains a small diary. The entries are all from previous guests. As you read over the thoughts and experiences from the past, take time to discuss the entry you would like to leave for the next visitors.

◆ *Romantic Alternative:* Across the street and up from Whale Watch Inn is the **NORTH COAST COUNTRY INN**, 34591 South Highway 1, (707) 884-4537 (Moderate), residing on a forested hillside with a view of the Pacific in the distance. The rooms have an assortment of French doors, private decks, large bay windows, fireplace, skylights, kitchenettes and comfortable (though dated) American furnishings. There is also a steamy outdoor hot tub for soaking tired spirits back to life. After having said all that, I have also to inform you that this attractive redwood home is located right next to Highway 1, which is hardly what you would call secluded and intimate. But at these prices and with this quality, it can be a fine place to stay on the coast.

ROTH RANCH, Gualala
37100 Old Stage Road
(707) 884-3124

Head north for 1 mile past the town of Gualala. Turn left on Pacific Woods Road. This road dead-ends at Old Stage Road, where you turn left. The ranch is 2 miles down the road.

Sonoma Coast's shoreline is the perfect cinematic setting for a gallop through surf and sand, especially if you know how to ride a horse. The waves splash against the horses' hooves as you ride effortlessly alongside someone you love. Sigh! Of course the clincher would be to stop along the way for a hearty lunch and a playful frolic in the foam. Given that scenario, it would be hard to pass up a trail ride at Roth Ranch. They have healthy, energetic horses for a journey that starts in dense forest and ends with romantic memories. In between, you can admire the long, empty beaches, eat lunch, and soak up some sun just by saddling up and trotting along the trail.

◆ *Romantic Note:* Horse rentals are by the hour, or you can request 3-hour excursions that include lunch or dinner on the beach.

ELK COVE INN, Elk
6300 South Highway
(707) 877-3321
Moderate

The inn is located 15 miles south of Mendocino on the west side of the road next to Highway 1.

This is one of those places I almost passed up. The unassuming facade of the main house looked plain and uninviting, and on top of that, I was tired and felt more like the Accidental Tourist than a romantic travel writer. Thank goodness, I have learned from past experience never to write a place off based solely on its outward appearance. Often I have found that what waits inside is more precious than anything I could have dreamed possible. Elk Cove Inn is such a place.

The guest rooms here are idyllic, spacious getaways that contain the kind of details lovers can appreciate. Some have bay windows, fireplaces, high-beamed ceilings, skylights, stained glass windows and private decks. There is even a handpainted tile shower in one of the cabins, with its own floor-to-ceiling view of the ocean. The views are stunning, with a sunset that will leave you speechless (which makes kissing that much easier). As if that weren't enough, Elk Cove Inn is renowned for its daily gourmet breakfast which leaves you satisfied until dinner. Did I forget to mention the driftwood-scattered beach below the inn? This is one place that you really should check out for yourselves.

HARBOR HOUSE, Elk

5600 South Highway 1
(707) 877-3203
Moderate

Just outside of Elk, on the west side of Highway 1.

The word "rustic" usually makes me nervous. It's hard to know exactly what is meant by the term. Rustic can conjure up images of knotty wood paneling, alcove sitting areas next to bay windows, crackling fireplaces and feather-down quilts three inches thick. It can also suggest paneling that is falling off the walls, drafty fireplaces that provide no warmth, and torn quilts that have seen better days. This inn by the sea is best described as a rustic sanctuary — of the first type and not anything like the second type. It is a place where the hours drift by and your mood is enhanced by the tranquility around you.

The inn is constructed of redwood, and resides on a bluff with awesome views of the water and the private beach below. The sweeping bay window from the dining room looks out onto haystack boulders and sea-worn rock arches that dot the ocean's surface. In this imposing setting, gourmet breakfasts and dinners are served to guests at the inn. The food is as pure as the location, with preference given to homegrown vegetables and herbs. You will find everything about Harbor House amorous and relaxing.

♦ *Romantic Note:* The moderate cost for staying here includes breakfast and dinner for 2. Now that's what I call good kissing information!

THE LEDFORD HOUSE, Albion
3000 North Highway 1
(707) 937-0282
Moderate to Expensive

Off Highway 1, south of Little River, on the west side of the road.

On a bluff with a spectacular view of the ocean, is one of the most elegant places for dinner along the coast. Inside, a crackling fireplace warms a charming array of linen-clad tables set with crystal and china. Candlelight flickers on whitewashed walls, creating a warm gentle feeling throughout. Even when the area is shrouded in fog (which occurs more often than some would like to admit), The Ledford House becomes still more cozy and inviting. There is little doubt that this place offers a touching environment for dining and kissing.

◆ *Romantic Note:* Be sure to call for reservations. This restaurant, like many others in this part of the world, is closed from Presidents Day until March 15th.

◆ *Romantic Option:* **LITTLE RIVER RESTAURANT**, 7750 North Highway 1, (707) 937-4945 (Inexpensive to Moderate) is probably one of the most unlikely locations for a restaurant, whether or not you are in the mood for romance. This obscure, tiny, thoroughly pleasing place to dine is attached to the back of a gas station. Yes, I said gas station, and yes, it is indeed special. A remarkably adept kitchen staff serves fresh fish, creatively prepared, at 2 seatings nightly to a cozy group of 7 tables. Plus, the reasonably priced entrees include soup and salad. Now this is what I call intimate!

ALBION RIVER INN, Albion

P.O. Box 100
(707) 937-1919
Inexpensive to Expensive

On the west side of Highway 1, near the town of Albion.

Albion River Inn was booked during my visit to the area, but I was able to see several of the rooms and I soon understood why they were so popular. After a long day of touring, if you want a secluded, beautiful place to watch the golden sunset turn the sky to fiery red as the ocean thunders against the shore below, this is the place to be. All of the rooms have superlative views. Or if you imagine yourselves soaking in a spa-size bathtub while a sizzling fire fills the room with an amber glow, many suites here have that feature as well. I may never forgive them for being booked! Well, at least their restaurant was open and the food was truly delicious and the view mesmerizing. Maybe I'll forgive them after all.

GLENDEVEN, Little River

Highway 1 in Little River
(707) 937-0083
Inexpensive to Expensive

On Highway 1, just south of Mendocino, look for the sign to Glendeven on the east side of the road. Turn right into the driveway.

This is country living at its best. The charming New Englandesque farmhouse is poised on verdant meadowland brushed by fresh ocean air. There are 12 unique guest suites at Glendeven and each is more engaging and provocative than the next. My first reaction was to utter a sigh of "Wow!" The entire bed & breakfast is replete with affectionate details and cozy furnishings. Fireplaces, balconies, redwood paneling, French doors leading to a sunny deck, large tiled bathrooms and spacious airy rooms are distributed throughout. Of special interest for those looking for heart-stirring accommodations are the Bayloft, Briar Rose and Pinewood suites. The Bayloft, in particular, is an incredible place to spend a weekend on the coast. If this room doesn't help set the mood, nothing will.

MENDOCINO

Four to five hours north of San Francisco on Highway 1.

If there is one place that is representative of coastal life in Northern California, it is Mendocino. The only words that appropriately fit this uncommon seaside town are "quaint" and "serene." Well, at least during the winter that's true. Other times of the year, "crowded"best characterizes this Cape Cod-style village. Quiet streets here are lined with whitewashed storefronts that house small specialty shops ripe for browsing and spending tourist dollars. There are also enviable bed & breakfasts that are frequently fully booked on weekends, months in advance. Of course, the main attraction is the view of the tranquil bay and rocky shoreline that surrounds Mendocino on all sides. In essence, this town is the yin and yang of getaway spots. The very elements that make it is so wonderful are also the reason why everyone and their cousins know about it. Still, there is off-season, when the crowds and sun are less present and the fog shrouds the area in a veil of misty white. But then that's what down comforters, fireplaces and snuggling close are there for.

◆ *Romantic Options:* The accommodations in Mendocino are numerous, varied and unique. My favorites are as follows:

AGATE COVE INN, 11201 North Lansing Street, (707) 937-0551 (Inexpensive to Expensive). One of the elements of a romantic place to stay is a view that overlooks a hypnotic seascape with the surf close enough to serenade you all night long. The Emerald and Obsidian rooms at Agate Cove make that fantasy come true. These oceanfront accommodations are cozy and comfortable. And the generous full breakfast served in the inn's extremely pleasant, window-outfitted dining room has a ringside view of the potent, rugged shoreline.

THE HEADLANDS INN, Howard and Albion Streets, (707) 937-4431 (Moderate) has 4 rooms that are an interesting blend of rustic and charming, and the views of the churning whitewater Pacific are exceptional. Plus each room has its own fireplace, and the full breakfasts, served directly to your door, are always exceptional.

MENDOCINO VILLAGE INN, 44860 Main Street, (707) 937-0246 (Inexpensive to Moderate) is an assortment of simple to charming guest rooms that have everything from private entrances to fireplaces, bay windows and canopied beds. Perhaps the highlight here is the gourmet breakfast of homemade cornbread, muffins, banana pancakes and quiches, which are some of the things you may find waiting for you in the morning.

SEA ROCK INN, (707) 937-5517 (Inexpensive to Moderate) is next door to Agate Cove and has the same sweeping view of the sea and rocky headlands. The rooms here range in style from basic and unassuming, to private cottages hidden by cypress trees, to rooms with spectacular water views and heat provided by Franklin stoves and woodburning fireplaces.

WHITEGATE INN, 499 Howard Street, (707) 937-4892 (Moderate) is a traditionally Victorian, extremely elegant bed & breakfast. The 6 guest rooms all have ocean or village views, some have fireplaces, and the beds are draped with thick, white down comforters. Observing the view of the bay from the huge parlor window is a delightful way to while away a morning, after partaking in the gracious continental breakfast served in the dining room.

THE GRAY WHALE BAR AND RESTAURANT, Mendocino
45020 Albion Street
(707) 937-5763
Moderate

As you turn west off Highway 1 onto Main Street, look for Lansing Street and turn right. The next block is Albion, where you turn left to the bar.

The epitome of Northwest dining and lounging is to be found here at The Gray Whale. The environment is a careful combination of country Victorian refinement and an appropriate amount of laid-back Californian spirit. Whoever handled this renovation knew what they were doing. It takes a great deal of skill to meld the warmth of the past with the finesse of the present and yet create the illusion that nothing has changed in 100 years. A substantial cobblestone fireplace fills the room with a burnished light that flickers warmly against oak paneling. The tables are placed far enough apart to provide for discreet conversation. A window-framed sunporch at the front of the lounge has seating that overlooks the water and street scene. Complementing this atmosphere is a menu of fresh fish, meats and produce that are exceptionally prepared and savory.

◆ *Romantic Suggestion:* The Gray Whale Bar is located on the ground floor of the **MACCALLUM HOUSE INN**, (707) 937-0289 (Inexpensive to Expensive) which is, to say the least, one of the most unusual bed & breakfasts I've ever seen. The meandering array of rooms and suites range in style from overly rustic to unusually romantic. For the purposes of kissing, the best units are The Barn and The Barn Apartment. The Barn has a massive stone fireplace, cozy sitting area and large picture window overlooking the bay. The Barn Apartment is similar, with the addition of a very sensual, very large bathroom. If those are not available, be sure to request a room that is as far away from the bar and restaurant as possible; otherwise you'll likely be listening to sounds of muffled laughter and clinking glasses.

MENDOCINO HEADLANDS AND BIG RIVER BEACH
STATE PARKS 💋💋💋💋

The coastal headlands and park surround Mendocino on all sides.

Perhaps more than any other attraction in Mendocino, the headlands and Big River State Park are the primary draws of this region. The protected, flawless curve of land is an easily accessible way to see, hear and feel nature in all its magnitude and glory. On a calm, sun-filled day, the glistening ocean will reveal hidden grottos, sea arches, tidepools and foamy white surf that encircles the rock-etched boundary of Mendocino. If you happen to be here December through March, you may see a school of whales making its way down the coast. On the days when the thick ocean fog enfolds the area in a white-gray cloak, this is still the prime place for exploring and daydreaming. Dress warmly and allow the cool mist to tingle against your cheeks as you taste the lightly salted air that wets your lips. Here you are with the wind sailing through your hair, the fog concealing your movements and someone special next to you.

◆ *Romantic Option:* **RUSSIAN GULCH STATE PARK,** (707) 937-5804 just north of Mendocino, off Highway 1, is a small campground with redwood-lined trails, rocky coves, water inlets, a quiet bay and campsites at water's edge. There aren't many tent spaces available here, so it is advisable to make reservations well in advance.

◆ *Second Romantic Option:***MACKERRICHER STATE PARK,** Fort Bragg, 3 miles north of Fort Bragg off Highway 1, is a wondrous assortment of nature's most attractive features — waterfalls at the end of forested trails, grass-covered headlands overlooking the Pacific, white sandy beaches, rolling dunes and haystack rocks where harbor seals spend the day sunning themselves. The most outstanding feature of this state park is its distance from Mendocino; the few miles make it less popular, and thus it has a definite kissing advantage.

> **"LOVE IS THE TRIUMPH OF**
> **IMAGINATION OVER INTELLIGENCE."**
>
> *H.L. Mencken*

WINE COUNTRY

THE NAPA AND SONOMA VALLEYS

From San Francisco take Highway 101 north to Highway 37 east. Highway 37 connects with Route 12 north through The Sonoma Valley or with Route 29 through The Napa Valley.

The hills in this holiday countryside are given over to vineyards and the succulent grapes they produce. Once you visit this region you will understand the vivacious, impetuous temperament that is the hallmark of the wine country, its robust, noblesse oblige regard for living life to its fullest. The boroughs and hamlets of the area are well-stocked with an enormous selection of bed & breakfasts, restaurants, spas, wine tastings, hot-air ballooning and the most remarkable picnic turf around. The roughest part of your travels here will be making a choice about where to concentrate your time. In line with the discriminating criteria of this book, we do earnestly rate the Napa and Sonoma valleys as brimming with the crème de la crème of romance.

♦ ***Romantic Consideration:*** The number of wineries scattered throughout these picturesque hills and valleys is staggering. Even if you were merely to sip your way in and out of the tasting rooms for a week, you would make only a nominal, intoxicating dent in the possibilities that exist here. Because this book is about sentiment and not about choosing a vintage wine, we've chosen a handful of the lesser known out-of-the-mainstream wineries we found to be the most appealing for embracing and tasting both the wine and each other.

SONOMA

From San Francisco take Highway 101 north to Highway 37 east. Highway 37 connects with Route 12 north to the town of Sonoma.

In spite of its popularity and tourist appeal, Sonoma is still an interesting place for a rendezvous. The village is wrapped around a village square shaded by sprawling oak trees and sculpted shrubbery. This central area is woven with flowering walkways, a gently flowing fountain, a duck pond, and park benches. Around the square's perimeter, branching out in all directions, is an array of shops, restaurants and wineries that have retained much of their original charm. Commercialism is softened to a purr instead of a roar.

Consider starting your day at a local espresso shop or bakery to gather all of the necessities for a breakfast picnic on the square's cool green lawn. The rest of your day can be spent gallivanting through the wineries and tasting rooms that line the surrounding lush hillsides and valleys. When evening arrives and you come back to where you began the day, there are enough gourmet dining options in Sonoma to keep both of you well occupied.

♦ *Romantic Warning:* Summer crowds in Sonoma can be overpowering all week long and unbearable on the weekends. Off-season is the best time to find a degree of solitude as well as comfortable weather conditions.

♦ *Romantic Option:* **TAYLOR'S OF SONOMA FLORIST SHOP**, (707) 938-1000 is a business that embodies the irresistible appeal of the past. The stone-mortared home stands alone on a side street just off the town square. The wrought-iron fence, wood stairway and stone threshold leading inside seem Lilliputian in dimension and style, and the bouquets of flowers in their multitude of colors and fragrances occupy every inch of available space.

SONOMA HOTEL'S RESTAURANT, Sonoma
110 West Spain Street
(707) 996-2996
Inexpensive

On the northwest corner of the plaza, at the intersection of West Spain Street and West First Street.

Consider the past and the lifestyle of the well-heeled West around the turn of the century. Whatever images you conjure up you'll find thriving at Sonoma Hotel's Restaurant. Visualize a lobby entered through two antique wooden doors. Once inside, you notice a chaise lounge next to a massive stone fireplace bordered by a mantel lined with hurricane lamps. A ceiling fan spinning overhead circulates aromas from deep within the kitchen. As you enter the dining area there are 3 separate seating areas from which to choose. The area closest to the front softly filters daylight through sheer curtains hanging from ceiling-tall windows. The rear section has a library theme with subdued lighting. Oak tables and paneling lend a rustic simplicity to the restaurant. Here your desire for good food, privacy and the past can be indulged.

♦ *Romantic Warning:* The hotel part of this landmark building is nice but a little too rustic. There are impressive, massive wood antique furnishings in some of the rooms, but they tend to overpower the space, which feels cramped and small. Five of the rooms have their own baths and are really quite charming, but the floors creak a little and the bathrooms are tiny.

♦ *Romantic Suggestion:* **THE VICTORIAN GARDEN INN**, 316 Napa Street, (707) 996-5339 (Inexpensive to Expensive) resides in the bucolic neighborhood of Sonoma. The home's ordinary exterior is Victorian, enveloped by a trellised walkway and garden. Behind the house is a swimming pool that takes up the entire backyard. Inside is where you will find the distinctive, comfortable accommo-dations — some with private entrances, wicker furnishings, fireplace, sitting areas and country-style antiques.

◆ *Second Romantic Suggestion:* **OVERVIEW FARM**, 15650 Arnold Drive, (707) 938-8574 (Inexpensive to Moderate) is far away from the mainstream of life in Sonoma. Situated on 5 acres of meadowland, the home is protected from the world by an arbor of large oak shade trees. The rooms are generous, with lofty ceilings, antiques and towering windows providing prominent views of the forests and vineyards that are interwoven through the valley and hills.

HACIENDA WINERY, Sonoma
P.O. Box 416
(707) 938-3220

At the Sonoma town square, turn right on East Napa Street and go 1 mile. At Seventh Street East, turn left and follow the signs on Castle Road.

If you've ever wondered which winery has the most romantic setting in the Napa/Sonoma Valley, Hacienda Winery may provide your answer. Its sensual setting is a tour de force of gardening skill and ageless beauty. The walk from the dusty unpaved parking area up to the stone cellar and tasting room is a stroll through venerable moss-covered trees and pinery. As the path narrows and turns, the city environs disappear behind you and ahead you face a vine-covered world. The grounds of the estate are etched with fragrant flowers, and strategically placed picnic tables provide exalted seating for gazing upon acre after acre of sinuous terrain. As far as the eye can see, rows of burgeoning grapevines are bordered with jade forest. A wildly flirtatious outing is here for the asking; your part is to do the asking and subsequent romancing.

◆ *Romantic Option:* In keeping with the spirit of your day spent stimulating your palate at the wineries, you'll want a dinner that is European and traditional. **MAGLIULO'S**, 691 Broadway, (707) 996-1031, (Inexpensive to Moderate) obliges with just that. It has a rustically pretty setting of wrought-iron and wood accented by pastel colors. Here you can relish incredible Italian cuisine and sensational desserts.

THE SILVERADO TRAIL

This stretch of highway follows the east side of the Napa Valley starting from the south, in the town of Napa, up north to the town of Calistoga.

Only two major roads traverse the Napa Valley: Highway 29 and the Silverado Trail. At some points these roads are separated by only one or two miles, but in spirit and atmosphere they are eons apart. Highway 29 is just that, a highway, encumbered with cars, billboards, tourists, gas stations and other "civilized" necessities. In contrast, the width and breadth of the Silverado Trail is a meandering drive through nature at its purest — contiguous, undulating hillsides endowed with a profusion of vineyards, forests and olive groves. As you map out your course through the wine country of Napa Valley, it would be a grievous mistake not to allow enough time to cruise along this absorbing roadway. The wineries that branch off in a network of backroads are less commercial and more personal than those that line the main road. Plus, when you do require provisions or restaurants, the towns of Napa, Yontville, Oakville, Rutherford, St. Helena and Calistoga are practically across the street.

PETRI'S, Napa
Monticello Road and Vichy Avenue
(707) 253-1455
Moderate to Expensive

On the east side of Napa, Trancas Road ends and turns into Highway 121, called Monticello Road. As you head towards Lake Berryessa, look for Vichy Avenue on your right. The restaurant is at this intersection.

Before you cast yourselves adrift on the backroads to find the sovereign wineries of this region, you may want to visit this amiable establishment filled with congenial charm and hearty pasta. The elfin cottage is so well-camouflaged by flowering gardens hugging close the vine-covered stone exterior, you may miss it completely. Two glass doors lead into the main dining areas, where wood-beamed ceilings, tile floors, wood tables and the rough-hewn stone walls all make a charming backdrop for your meal. Sauce-laden pastas accompany continental dinners that are sure to please the most discriminating elfin gourmets.

♦ **Romantic Suggestion:** Personally, I find the town of Napa too industrial and citified to be considered a romantic destination, especially when there are so many other quaint delightful villages to recommend. But there is a bed & breakfast in Napa that is just too outstanding and too exceedingly romantic for me not to include it. **THE OLD WORLD INN**, 1301 Jefferson Street, (707) 257-0112 (Moderate to Expensive) is beautiful and inviting. Each room is unique, with features that include private decks, canopied beds, large bay and ceiling windows and comfortable furnishings. There is also a huge outdoor hot tub in the backyard. The buffet breakfast and evening wine-and-hors d'oeuvre fest are both generous and superb.

OAK KNOLL INN, Napa
2200 East Oak Knoll Avenue
(707) 255-2200
Expensive

Take Highway 29 heading north. Just outside the town of Napa, turn right onto Oak Knoll Avenue and continue about 2 miles to the inn.

The rooms here are the most impressive I've seen anywhere, plus the location is as far removed from the maddening crowd as you could ever hope for. The inn's stone entrance and wrought-iron gate only suggest the splendor that lies inside. Once you enter the courtyard area, where the two wings of suites surround the crystal aqua-blue swimming pool, you will realize that you have stumbled upon a tranquil retreat. Besides the handful of other guests, there is nothing else for miles around but the fertile vineyards and lush meadows and woodlands of the Napa Valley. The interior of each suite has a remarkable 17-foot-tall wood-beamed ceiling, a floor-to-ceiling draped window, fireplaces set into an inlaid stone wall, gorgeous bathrooms with marble floors, and French doors that open onto the inner courtyard. If I were you, I wouldn't hesitate on this one, it is that special.

♦ *Romantic Suggestion:* **FRENCH LAUNDRY**, Yontville, 6640 Washington Street, (707) 944-2380 (Expensive) is an appealing restaurant housed in a brick, two-story, affectionately renovated country building where superlative meals are prepared and served. Reputed to be one of the finest in the Napa Valley, it is also one of the most charming.

VICHON WINERY, Oakville
1595 Oakville Grade
(707) 944-2811

From Highway 29 turn west on Trinity Road to the winery.

The view from up here is a gorgeous sylvan expanse of neatly arrayed vineyards blanketing the sloping hills as they surge down into the valley below. In the distance, forested peaks go on for as far as the eye can see. There is a picnic area on a knoll overlooking this bewitching landscape. As long as you're in this setting, you might as well indulge in a very Californian kind of afternoon and pack a picnic basket that includes a vintage bottle of wine, fresh cheeses and sweet, ripe fruit.

♦ *Romantic Note:* Speaking of gourmet Californian-style picnic lunches, the absolute best place anywhere for 100 miles around is the **OAKVILLE GROCERY**, on Highway 29 in Yontville. This intriguing collection of patés, cheeses, olives, cured meats and salads are all luscious to look at, delectable to eat and outrageously expensive to buy. This is gourmet heaven, except for the pricetags.

♦ *Romantic Suggestion:* **DOMAINE CHANDON**, California Drive, off Highway 29 in Yontville (Expensive) is considered by many to be the most beautiful dining setting in the entire Bay Area. Well, I have to agree that the inlaid stone walls and arched wood-beamed ceiling and doorways are all luxurious. The only obstacles to an intimate dining atmosphere are the room's large size, its popularity and its poor acoustics which make for a somewhat noisy evening. It is still a lovely place to dine, though, and the food is very good and often superb, and the champagne is superior. If you schedule yourselves here before prime eating hours, you're likely to find the experience rapturous.

AUBERGE DU SOLEIL RESTAURANT AND LOUNGE, Rutherford   💋💋💋💋
180 Rutherford Hill Road
(707) 963-1211
Expensive to Very Expensive

From Highway 29, just after the town of Rutherford, turn right on Zinfandel Lane. This lane intersects with the Silverado Trail, where you turn right again. Look for Rutherford Hill Road and turn left up the hill.

High above the Napa Valley, perched atop a ridge, Auberge du Soleil has a commanding perspective of the entire countryside. Ensconced in hills with flourishing olive groves, the restaurant and lodge integrate so well with the landscape that they seem to be organically linked. Walls of cream-colored stucco, light pine-paneled ceilings, wooden tables and a Spanish-style hearth all add to this effect. The dining room and lounge are designed to supply premium viewing pleasure from every nook and corner of the restaurant. The tables in the lounge are positioned near a fireplace large enough to generate ample warmth. A late-evening visit will allow you to drink in the watercolor hues of the day yielding to night. Whether you indulge in a dining adventure here or simply toast each other in the bar, the potential for romance is more than likely — it's guaranteed.

◆ **Romantic Suggestion:** Rising above Auberge du Soleil is **RUTHERFORD HILL WINERY**, P.O. Box 388, 200 Rutherford Hill Road, (707) 963-9694. This is a heart-tugging spot to bring a picnic with your own tempting specialties for a leisurely lunch and wine-tasting event. Spread your blanket under the shade of a sprawling tree overlooking the splendid view of the valley. Then as the cool of evening approaches, you can saunter down to Auberge du Soleil and toast the beginnings of an amorous night.

◆ **Second Romantic Suggestion: CAYMUS KITCHEN**, which is part of Rancho Caymus Inn, Rutherford, P.O. Box 78, (707) 963-1777 (Inexpensive) prepares one of the more piquant breakfasts you will find anyplace in the valley. The Spanish atmosphere and decor are cozy and congenial. The tiled floors, wood tables, colorful tapestries and gracious service are all a pleasure. Personally, my favorite meal of the day is breakfast, and the more loving and leisurely it is, all the better. Be sure that one of you tries "Caymus Eggs" — scrambled eggs with creamy rich guacamole, cheese and chiles, presented with a mimosa cocktail.

VILLA ST. HELENA
2727 Sulphur Springs Avenue
(707) 963-2514
Expensive to Very Expensive

Head north on Highway 29 (St. Helena Highway). After the town of Rutherford and just before you enter St. Helena, turn west onto Sulphur Springs Avenue. Follow this road up and around to a wood corral fence that may or not be open, and continue up the drive to the villa.

Most bed & breakfasts are older homes that have been transformed to offer visitors the pleasures of homey living with a sprinkling of extras that make you feel spoiled and slightly hedonistic. There are as many different ways of achieving that as there are bed & breakfasts.

What makes Villa St. Helena so special is that both these ingredients are abundantly present. There are only 3 guest rooms, located at opposite wings of this architecturally renowned Spanish mansion. The 20-acre estate is situated on a hillcrest overlooking Napa Valley. From within, the grand interior becomes your exclusive residence, and the sensuous grounds and courtyard become your playground.

As you awaken from a lazy nap in your private suite, you may want to slip into your swimsuit, pour a glass of wine and lounge by the pool for an afternoon of carefree fun. At twilight you can explore the restaurants of St. Helena, returning to the opulence of your weekend villa while the evening is still young. If you happen to be in the mood to spend an evening or a weekend in the lap of luxury, this is it.

◆ *Romantic Suggestion:* Some of the more popular or roadside wineries in this region get very crowded and busy. They are hardly conducive to the traditional toast with a clink of glasses, arms entwined at the elbow and a sip from each other's glass. But you can get up and away from the throngs by going to **CAIN CELLARS**, St. Helena, 3800 Langtry Road, (707) 963-1616. Besides being well off the beaten track, they allow visitors by appointment only. To get here, follow Spring Mountain Road, which snakes its way up into the hills behind St. Helena. Once here you will be dazzled by the stellar, all-encompassing view of the valley, arched hillsides covered in bountiful grapevines and, on a very clear day, a glimpse of the Pacific Ocean some 50 miles away.

RESTAURANT TERRA, St. Helena

1345 Railroad Avenue
(707) 963-8931
Moderate to Expensive

From the town of St. Helena, take Highway 29 going north. Turn right at Hunt Street. Just before the railroad tracks, turn left at Railroad Avenue. Look for the restaurant on the west side of the street.

To my way of thinking, antiques and icons of the past do not automatically induce thoughts or actions that lead to kissing (or even hugging, for that matter). But with the adept blending of days-gone-by with appropriate contemporary flourishes, *voilà*, you have all the romantic atmosphere you could ever need. Restaurant Terra has that welcome mix of yesterday and today. This 100-year-old building has a noble yet heartwarming quality. As you enter the iron gate and move past the stone exterior, prepare yourselves for a walk into provincial pleasure. It will be like setting foot in a miniature French castle. The wood beams that loom overhead, burnt-red tile floor and stone walls are complemented by magnificent tapestries, Oriental rugs and contemporary paintings. This is your setting for an award-winning gastronomic dining affair. The menu itself is an ingenious assortment of fresh fish and game, prepared in rich yet delicate sauces.

BURGESS CELLARS, St. Helena

1108 Deer Park Road
(707) 963-4766

Take the Silverado Trail going north. Turn right onto Deer Park Road. As you wind up the mountain towards the town of Angwin, look on the left side of the road for the entrance to Burgess Cellars.

There are many reasons why you should visit one winery rather than another. If you are a consummate oenophile you may be lured by the exceptional quality of the grapes at a particular estate, or the rare vintage at an established vineyard. But it is also a treat when you become acquainted with the offerings of a small up-and-coming winery and can take pride in your secret discovery. All this and more are sublime reasons to seek out Burgess Cellars in the hills of Napa Valley. In addition to its winemaking craft, Burgess is famous for some of the most striking views of the Napa countryside. Your feelings and tastebuds will soar to new heights here.

♦ *Romantic Suggestion:* The drive up to Burgess Cellars along **DEER PARK ROAD** is stupendous. As you weave up this twisting road, there are marvelous vistas of the ravines and dells below.

FOREST MANOR, Angwin
415 Cold Springs Road
(707) 965-3538
Moderate to Expensive

Take the Silverado Trail past the town of St. Helena. Turn right onto Deer Park Road at the red blinking light. The road winds up through the hills for 5½ miles to Angwin. At Cold Springs Road turn left. When the road forks take a right. (If you take the left fork you will dead-end at Los Posados State Forest.) Forest Manor is at the end of Cold Springs Road.

Forest Manor is the ideal destination for a weekend sojourn. Here you can renew your relationship with each other and with the good life. This English Tudor estate is located on the outskirts of Napa Valley, backed by boundless woodlands and a neighboring 100-year-old winery. This special domicile has exotic furnishings from the Orient and an open staircase that ascends four flights to two of the three guest rooms. Your suite will have its own breakfast nook, a roaring fireplace, comfortable furnishings and the relaxing quiet of nature all around. A country breakfast is graciously provided. In the dewy morning or under the stars at night you can submerge yourselves in the outdoor whirlpool. During the heat of midday there is also a 53-foot-long swimming pool for more invigorating recreation. At the end of your stay, consider burying a treasure chest with mementos of your visit — perhaps a bottle of wine, a menu from a favorite restaurant, or love notes all wrapped for hiding in the forest. Then on your return visit, you can retrace your steps, dig up your memories and create anew the treasures of the past.

SCHRAMSBURG VINEYARDS, Calistoga (707) 942-4558

On the west side of Highway 29, just south of Calistoga, look for a small sign that signals the turnoff for the winery.

To say the least, there are many wonderful vineyards in the Napa Valley. One of the more distinctive and beautiful is to be found at Schramsburg. This 100-year-old estate, located in the highlands of Napa Valley, is a beacon of historical interest. The stone buildings of the winery are located far enough away from the traffic of the main road to provide quiet refuge. Because only private tours are allowed, your introduction to the world of champagne will be sparklingly intimate. After you roam through the labyrinth of underground cellars that were tunneled into the rocky ground years ago, be certain to leave enough time to stop at the wine-tasting room. By this point you will have learned almost all the secrets of *méthode champenoise*, so you can purchase your own bit of effervescent history to share.

◆ *Romantic Option:* There are picnic grounds at the winery, or you can wander off to **BOTHE NAPA VALLEY STATE PARK** next door. During the week, especially off-season, this area is not well traveled, so you are almost guaranteed to find yourselves alone with nature and each other.

ONCE IN A LIFETIME (Hot Air Balloon Rides), Calistoga
P.O. Box 795
(707) 942-6541
Very Expensive

As you enter the town of Calistoga from Highway 29, turn right on Lincoln Avenue. This is the main street. Just past Washington Street you will notice the parking lot for the airport, where your pilot will meet you.

If you're thinking that a mere balloon ride sounds like a capricious and frivolous enterprise, you're right. That's exactly what it is — a tingling, exciting, stimulating way to spend an early morning. Your excursion commences at sunrise, when the air is still and cool (yes, that means somewhere between 5 and 8 a.m.). As you step into the balloon's gondola, your eyes will gape at the towering, billowing fabric overhead, and your heart will begin to flutter with wild expectation. Once aloft, as the wind guides your craft above the countryside, the world will seem more peaceful than you ever thought possible. You will also be startled by the sunrise from this vantage point; daylight awakens the hills with new vigor and warmth. After your flight, a poolside champagne brunch awaits you at a nearby hotel. "Carried away" will suddenly take on a new meaning that the two of you will keep in your hearts forever.

◆ *Romantic Note:* A caress while floating over the world on a cloudless summer morning can be a thoroughly heavenly experience. There are many hot-air balloon companies in this part of the world. Check with your innkeeper or the telephone directory to find the balloon business nearest you.

FOOTHILL HOUSE, Calistoga
3037 Foothill Boulevard
(707) 942-6933
Moderate to Expensive

Head north on Highway 29 to the town of Calistoga. Stay on 29, which will become 128 after you cross Lincoln Avenue. On the west side of the road, just past the town of Calistoga, 1 block north of Petrified Forest Road, Foothill House will be on your left.

When I first saw this country home, I drove right by it. My initial impression was not the best. The nondescript frame house with its highway frontage disappointed me. I thought: *"This can't be romantic!"* But lessons learned in the past made me turn around and go back. Once again I found that I must never judge a book by its cover. The outside of Foothill House gives no indication of the rapture and ease that waits inside.

The sizable rooms overflow with everything your sentimental hearts could desire: a four-poster bed, a patchwork quilt, a private sundeck and a fireplace stacked with logs waiting for a hearthside sip of sherry. There is also a newly built separate cottage with a Jacuzzi bathtub and fireplace. If that isn't enough, after a full day of sweeping your way through the wineries and health spas of this county, you'll return to find the bed neatly turned down, fluffy fresh towels, wine, and the *pièce de resistance* — a ceramic canister of hot, chewy, chocolate chip cookies. (Yes, cookies and wine sound a bit odd, but you have to taste these phenomenal little gems before you form an opinion.) In the morning, depending on your mood, an impeccable breakfast can be served in your room or in the glass-enclosed patio. As you linger over the last morsel, you will be revitalized for an encore performance of the day before.

♦ *Romantic Suggestion:* **CALISTOGA INN,** 1250 Lincoln Avenue, (707) 942-4101 (Moderate) is a charming restaurant with an elegant rustic atmosphere. This is a perfect place for couples who need a certain amount of dining intimacy after a long day at the spas. The specialty here is delicious fresh fish, creatively prepared.

SILVER ROSE INN, Calistoga
351 Rosedale Road
(707) 942-9581
Moderate to Expensive

From the Silverado Trail, just outside of Calistoga, turn north onto Rosedale Road.

Silver Rose Inn is a fabulous bed & breakfast located a discreet distance from Calistoga. It is far enough away from the spa-scene, which can get a bit crowded, that you'll feel elated about staying here. This large, newly constructed estate is spread over an oak-studded knoll that has been lovingly landscaped to blend with the nearby foothills and leas. The hallmark of this place is an impressive rock garden with a flowing waterfall that spills into a huge stone-etched swimming pool adjoining the capacious Jacuzzi. And, of course, framing the entire backyard are hundreds of striking rosebushes that give the inn its proud appellation. The rooms are not quite as outstanding as the common areas, but they are indeed nice and inviting. All are quite comfortable and attractively furnished, and they have views of the nearby vineyards.

INTERNATIONAL SPA, Calistoga
P.O. Box 856
(707) 942-6122

I could be wrong, but I believe that there is no place else in the United States quite like Calistoga, California. The entire town is dedicated to the rejuvenation of the body and spirit through an ingenious variety of treatments. The services at most spas range from a tranquilizing, peaceful massage to an invigorating rubdown that will knead away any anxiousness you may have brought with you from the city. The staff at International Spa also do foot reflexology and acupressure massage. Though they explained what the benefits are of these two techniques, I can only tell you that it felt great and I didn't want them to stop.

As time slinked by, I was taken to another room where I was introduced to the organic mudbaths. This is something you can do side by side with a loved one. If I fully describe the mudbath, you may decide not to try it; I know I didn't want to when I read about it. But take my word for it, after sitting for over an hour in something I used to get in trouble for as a kid, it was the most amazing physical sensation I have experienced. It's not vaguely romantic, but afterwards you'll feel that all you want to do is melt into your loved one's arms.

There are other services here you can experiment with — like facials, herbal blanket wraps (also a side-by-side service), enzyme baths, mineral baths and on and on. The longer I was there, the more I came to understand the fascination people have for this place. I also realized how two people sharing such an experience could feel closer to each other than ever before. I think for the first time in my life every muscle in my body was in a blissful state. I'd go back and do this again — next time for an entire week.

♦ *Romantic Note:* There are a half dozen or so spas in the Calistoga area. Some are associated with hotels, but most of the accommodations at these places are mediocre and small. You can enjoy the services of most of the spas without having to stay there. For tender cuddling after a day at the spa, find your way back to one of the idyllic bed & breakfasts this area has to offer.

THE GRAPE LEAF INN, Healdsburg
539 Johnson Street
(707) 433-8140
Inexpensive to Moderate

Head north on Highway 12. Take the second Healdsburg exit (Healdsburg Avenue) and turn left on Grant Street. Two blocks east is Johnson Street.

Many places I passed through on my tour of the wine country were not what I would call romantic. Yet every now and again there was a surprise that kept my search entertaining. This kissing place in Healdsburg was one of those surprises. In an otherwise ordinary suburban group of houses, my attention was diverted by a conspicuously purple bed & breakfast called The Grape Leaf Inn. You have to see it for yourselves. This inn is a winsome and welcome combination of eccentricity and solace. There are 7 suites with 7 personalized baths in this brightly refurbished Queen Anne-style home. From the outside it's hard to imagine that there is room for one, much less seven, rooms. But not only is there more than enough space, the accommodations are ample, the decor jubilant and the design fascinating. There are skylights, multicolored windows, separate sitting areas, whirlpool baths for two, and hardwood floors covered by Oriental rugs. An overnight stay here will be a surprising concoction of fun and good old-fashioned romance.

◆ **Romantic Note:** For intimate dining in this part of the wine country, check out **MADRONA MANOR RESTAURANT,** Healdsburg, 1001 Westside Road, (707) 433-4231 (Moderate). This landmark restaurant is considered to be one of the finest in the area, and the setting, without doubt, is definitely romantic.

HEALDSBURG INN, Healdsburg
116 Matheson Street
(707) 433-6991
Moderate

In the town of Healdsburg, just one block east of Healdsburg Avenue, on the park green.

I was a bit skeptical when I entered the lobby area of Healdsburg Inn. This narrow ground floor, where the gift shop is located, was attractive but not appealing. Once I walked up the grand staircase that led to the bed & breakfast area on the second floor, I was enthralled with what I saw. The rooms encircled an enormous mezzanine. Each suite has a private bath, some have fireplaces, and all were decorated affectionately in American antiques, thick down comforters, firm canopied beds, and cozy sitting areas trimmed in pastel colors and textured country fabrics. The rooftop garden and solarium is the charming setting for a hearty, savory breakfast and afternoon tea served with cake and cookies that are creamy and richly decadent.

◆ *Romantic Alternative:* **BELLE DU JOUR INN**, 16276 Healdsburg Avenue, (707) 433-7892 (Moderate) is situated on 6 acres of rolling hills lined with vineyards and profuse greenery. As you enter the driveway you will see white cottages nestled amidst tall trees that oversee the majestic landscape. Each guest room has an assortment of amenities that are hard to choose among. One has a fireplace, whirlpool tub and French doors that open to a trellised deck, another has high vaulted ceilings, woodburning stove and whirlpool tub. Breakfast in the morning is a bountiful affair that can be enjoyed on the garden deck or in the privacy of your own room.

RUSSIAN RIVER WINE ROAD
Highway 128 to Chalk Hill Road

*From Healdsburg follow Healdsburg Avenue north till it becomes Alexander
Valley Road. Follow this road to Highway 128 and turn south. Highway
128 will branch off to the east; to the west is Chalk Hill Road.*

The handful of wineries along this backwoods road are set apart
from the rest of the Napa Valley by their isolation and beauty. Coiling
through the hillsides and ravines, your path crisscrosses the tributaries
and creeks of the Russian River. Along the way, the vineyards,
redwoods and forests take turns revealing their distinctive virtues and
profiles. Whenever you see a sign along here that says "Winery," it
means you're invited to stop and rest for a bit under the shade of a
tree or in the coolness of a cellar's tasting room.

"TO BE A LOVER IS NOT TO MAKE LOVE,

BUT TO FIND A NEW WAY TO LIVE."

Paul La Cour

PERSONAL DIARY

This is the section just for the two of you. Here is where you can keep your own record of the romantic, fulfilling moments you've shared together — where you went, what you discovered, the occasion celebrated and whatever else you want to remember long after the event has passed. When you're feeling nostalgic, that's the time to read aloud from these personalized pages, to share them as a gift to one another, creating a quiet, at-home magic moment.

"LOVE DOESN'T MAKE THE WORLD GO AROUND —

IT'S WHAT MAKES THE RIDE WORTHWHILE."

Franklin P. Jones

> "HE GAVE HER A LOOK
> YOU COULD HAVE SPREAD ON A WAFFLE."
> *Ring Lardner*

"LIFE IS JUST ONE FOOL THING AFTER ANOTHER;
LOVE IS JUST TWO FOOL THINGS AFTER EACH OTHER."

Anonymous

"IN LITERATURE AS IN LOVE, WE ARE ASTONISHED
AT WHAT IS CHOSEN BY OTHERS."

André Maurois

INDEX

Alphabetical Listing by Area

EAST OF SAN FRANCISCO

NORTH OF SAN FRANCISCO

WINE COUNTRY

Towns Included

"DON'T MISS LOVE, IT'S AN INCREDIBLE GIFT."

Leo F. Buscaglia

YOUR OWN PERSONAL DIARY